AF447860

Mother Courage
and her children

Mother Courage
and her children

Bertolt Brecht

Translated by Tom Leonard

Bertolt Brecht, Mutter Courage und ihre Kinder.
Mother Courage and Her Children. Translated by Tom Leonard.
© Bertolt-Brecht-Erben / Suhrkamp Verlag 1989.

Preface copyright Tom Leonard Literary Estate.

This edition published by the Tom Leonard Literary Estate from an original
by Smokestack books
ISBN 9798462453076

Preface

'This war will never go away' is the last line of the last verse of the peripatetic Song of Mother Courage that spans *Mother Courage and her Children* from within the opening scene until the drama's closing words. At present in the early part of the twenty-first century the war is called 'The War on Terror'. As template for the war that never goes away Brecht writing in the late Thirties deployed in his play the Thirty Years' War of the early seventeenth century.

It is a useful template. It traverses Europe in and out of countries till one might be unsure which country one is in; the participating cast is multinational. So, in fact, is Mother Courage's family. Which is to say, what does nationality and country matter in this war that goes on forever? Nationality is an irrelevance, nationalism an excuse, patriotism an exhortation. And so is religion, in this 'religious' war. Everything is agenda. The language, integral core of the whole, is hopelessly agenda-corrupted. In a world, and a drama, cancered by the insatiable drive for profit be it in cheese or arms, language must be likewise cancered too: the only compassionate person on the stage, the only person who is capable of instinctively loving children from the heart and of sacrificing her own life for others, is Kattrin – and she cannot speak. As Mother Courage remarks, by the time of her death Kattrin has a scar wound on the face – so she cannot even properly market her own body.

Mother Courage herself is both spirit of survival and spirit of war itself. This is why she is such a great character, and one of the reasons why this is such a great play. She will not be pinned down, she is alive and alone remains alive at the end walking from the stage in survival at the back of the troops walking onwards in war. But the play like all literature is made of language; and the true hero of this play is the language in which it was written. But it is an anti- hero.

Brecht's Hamburg like Scotland's Glasgow was a working-class heavily industrialised northern European city. If you want to see what Glasgow would have looked like had it been subject to mass bombing, look at the photographs of Hamburg at the end of the Second World War. But it is not just in stone one could find comparable structures: Brecht's Hamburg could have comparable social structures, and at its heart, comparable class structures that could be reflected in comparable linguistic structures.

Commentators have written of the play's essential untrans- latability, the idiomatic Hamburg speech having been essayed in attempted Lancashire (Willetts) or pacy Brooklyn-sounding American (Kushner). Both have their merits. But the translation I myself learned most from was by the American H.R. Hays, whose *Mother Courage* marked the play's first appearance in print in the 1941 *New Directions in Prose and Poetry*. H.R. Hays also translated an anthology *Selected Poems* of Brecht (Harcourt Brace, 1947) which remains for me the most sustainedly successful attempt to convey Brecht's ballad narratives in English. This book has been reissued in paperback.

To have Mother Courage speak in the working class idiom of Western Scotland and urban Glasgow speech was a natural choice for a Glasgow writer like myself. The language could offer phrases and turns of speech, sardonic humour and class-rooted comment to parallel, I would hope, the original Hamburg. That at any rate was the aim, always bearing in mind that it was Brecht, and Brecht's play alone, that must be scrupulously kept to the fore. Such of the songs as I found had been set to music by Brecht's collaborator Paul Dessau, I translated whilst listening to the songs in earphones, the matter being to establish syllabic numeric congruence with the sung German. Again, translating rhymed verse as some of the songs here can offer specific translation problems – whether or not to go with free verse, sense versus sound and so on: in the Chaplain's 'Song of the Hours' I found the best result for me was in moving from an abab structure to aaab.

I have kept the stage directions preceding each scene to a bare minimum. It is Brecht's play itself that with the passage of years has become template for this war that never goes away. The place and time of the play's occurrence is the place and time in which the drama, and this endless war – on stage and yet outside the theatre – presently occurs.

Tom Leonard
Glasgow 8 December 2013

Scene One

Country road near a town. Recruiting officer and Sergeant standing shivering.

Recruiting Officer How can they expect me to drum up a company of squaddies in a dump like this. Know what I keep thinking Sergeant. I could do myself in so I could.

Four companies a men, that's what the General says he's after. Four companies by the twelfth. And they're so friendly the natives round here, you'd be scared to shut your eyes at night in case they stole them out your head.

Suppose you do manage to find some bloke who's neither constitutionally chesty nor got legs riddled with varicose veins. Give him a few drinks down the pub to soften him up and get him signed on. Job done, he tells you he's just stepping outside a sec to the lav. Out you go yourself a minute later, he's nowhere to be seen. Off, faster than a greyhound out a trap.

You can't rely on a man's word any more Sergeant. Loyalty, faith, honour, all that's a thing of the past. Makes you give up hope for the whole human race.

Sergeant A bloody good war, that's what they need round here. That would sort things out. Too much of this peace malarkey all over the place. Peace doesn't sort things out. Takes a war to do that.

Trouble with peace is, it's got no system to it. No methodology. What's the point of your armaments if they're lying around not doing any good?

Even the way they eat's all higgledy piggledy. You'll see somebody with a piece of bread and cheese and they've maybe got *lard* on smeared on it. What kind of system is that?

How many warhorses has this town got? How many young chaps of army age?

They won't know. Nobody's bothered to count them. Not a census. Not a system. That's your 'peace' for you.

Know what? I've been in places they hadn't had a decent war for seventy years. Seventy years. You'll never guess. The people didn't have ID's. They weren't even on a national filing system! How could they know who they were without ID's?

War's what you need. Gets people listed and enlisted, their goods and chattels in the filing system. You can tot it all up, the folk, the animals–you can take it all away. That's war.

No system, no methodology – that's Peace.

Recruiting Officer You're right there.

Sergeant Same as with anything half decent, you've your work cut out to get a decent war under way. Once it's started you can relax there's no stopping it. They're all like cardsharks afraid to throw in their hand in case they lose. The same ones that were once telling you they didn't want to join up in case a war broke out. That's your average citizen. Always afraid of change.

Sound of jew's harp. A covered cart drawn by two young men comes in. On it sit Mother Courage and her daughter Kattrin.

Recruiting Officer Hold on here's an army stores wagon, two young blokes hauling it with a couple of women on top.

Get them to stop. If there's no result here I'm offsky. Spring my arse, it's freezing.

Mother Courage *Enters, calling:* Mornin, Sergeant.

Sergeant *Blocking the way.* Good morning to you. Who the hell are you?

Mother Courage Decent businessfolk.

Sings:

hawd yer wheesht there stoap yer drum
it's mother courage this way come
oh have yer squaddies halt and buy
new boots and claes an aw forbye!
flearidden sojers who love their loot
still want the guns they need tae shoot
but how does yer squaddie march tae fight
in scabby boots that's faur too tight?

    It's springtime noo! move on your way
    the snaw's aw gone. the deid
    lie deid but you that huvny died as yet
    the powers that be, they still do need.

wi no one sausage for to eat
yer squaddie'll fight till he faws deid
gie him some forage on his feet
a drap a beer, wi a hunk a breid!
'spite clapped oot guns 'spite empty stomachs
yer top brass still say aw is well
oh get your squaddies fit and well here!
march them fit tae the jaws o hell!

    It's springtime noo! move on your way
    the snaw's aw gone. the deid lie deid
    but you that huvny died as yet
    the powers that be, they still do need.

Sergeant Where are you motley lot coming from?

Eilif Two Regiment.

Sergeant Papers.

Mother Courage What are you talking about papers.

Swiss Cheese This is Mother Courage!

Sergeant Never heard of her. What's she doing with a name like that.

Mother Courage They call me Mother Courage cause once I thought the business was going broke and I drove right through a missile bombardment carrying fifty loaves. They were gettin mouldy you see I had to get them sold…

Sergeant Cut the cackle. Papers. Let me see them.

Mother Courage *Rummaging among papers in tin box and climbs down from wagon.* Just a minute… just a minute… See there's a good family Bible, I always wanted some decent paper to wrap my cucumbers and wet vegetables in. Very fine rice paper you know Sergeant. Quality. Here's a roadmap of…. God knows I'll never reach that place might as well fling that away... This here. You know that's a qualified vet guaranteeing our horse in sound health and totally free of mortal disease. Very desirable document that would you not agree? Pity the horse dropped dead that animal cost me a fair whack. Least it would have if I'd paid for it, thank goodness I never got round to that. Are these all the papers you need?

Sergeant Are you pulling my leg? Where's the road licence? Don't try any nonsense, you know you need a road licence.

Mother Courage Less of the smutty talk before my weans if you don't mind. I wouldny pull anything of yours sergeant you know that perfectly well. The only licence I have is ma respectable honest face, that's aye been good enough for Two Regiment and if you canny see that I canny help you. You needny put a stamp on it either.

Recruiting Officer Plain insubordination this. Discipline. That's what this army is crying out for. Discipline.

Mother Courage I'd say sausages. Lorne or links, it doesny matter. A good feed a sausages.

Sergeant What. Is. Your. Name.

Mother Courage Anna. Anna Fierling.

Sergeant So you're all the Fierling family.

Mother Courage No, I'm the only Fierling.

Sergeant Aren't these your children?

Mother Courage So. Why do they all have to be called the same? *Pointing to older son* Eilif, he's a Noyocki, at least his father was a Koyocki, or maybe it was Moyocki. Eilif remembers his father well. Only it's not actually his dad he remembers it's a Frenchman with a pointy beard. But he does have his father's brains though. Can lay out a big farmer on his back with one thump. We've all got our own names here.

Sergeant You've all got a different name?

Mother Courage A bit slow on the uptake are we Sergeant?

Sergeant *Pointing to the younger son:* I suppose this one's the son of a Chinaman.

Mother Courage Don't show your prejudices. He's Swiss.

Sergeant Came after the Frenchman did he?

Mother Courage What Frenchman? Stop mixing everything up or we'll be here all day. He's Swiss, I called him Feyos, though that wasn't after his Dad, his dad had some other name. An army engineer his dad was. Alcoholic.

Swiss cheese smile and nod. Kattrin smiles too.

Sergeant How come his name's Feyos?

Mother Courage Use your loaf. My man was Hungarian when Feyos came on the scene. He wasny that bothered too about Feyos turning up. Awful trouble that man had with his liver. Him a teetotaller he always maintained. The soul of honesty he was. The boy's just like him.

Sergeant But you said he *wasn't* his father!

Mother Courage So. I only said Feyos is just like him. I call him Swiss Cheese.

Pointing to her daughter: And this is Kattrin, Kattrin Haupt. Her dad was a German.

Sergeant Some family this I must say.

Mother Courage We've been all over the place, us and this wagon.

Sergeant I'm taking a note of all this. You've come a long way. What are you doing here?

Mother Courage I couldny hang around waiting till the war's made up its mind to come to me could I?

Sergeant And you two Jacob and Esau oxes. Does your mummy never let you out of harness?

Eilif Mum. Will I thump this fucker?

Mother Courage Let it go Eilif. Now my fine upstanding soldiery, how are you in the guns department? Couple of nice pistols maybe? Or a belt for your breeks? That belt looks a teenzie bit on the frayed side Sergeant.

Sergeant I've something a bit more to the point on my mind. A fine upstanding pair of lads you have here. Strong as birch trees, broadchested with it... What's manly quality like this doing out of army uniform?

Mother Courage *Quickly:* No way you're gettin sons of mine in the army.

Sergeant There's good money to be had. And fame is the spur. Minding the shoe shop is women's work.

To Eilif: Come on you. Are you a man or a mouse?

Mother Courage He's a mouse. Stamp your foot and he'll run away.

Sergeant Headlong into battle I'd reckon. *Goes to lead him away.*

Mother Courage Get your hands off him! He's not signing up!

Recruiting Officer He swore at me. We'll have to settle this jackets off.

Eilif Never mind Mum. I'll pulverise this arsehole.

Mother Courage Stay where you are. Always spoiling for a fight you.
To officer: He's a knife on him you know, my son's a dab hand with a blade..

Recruiting Officer I'll take that off him like sweeties from a wean. Come on man.

Mother Courage The Colonel will get hearing about this and the pair of you are goany find yourselves in the military jail. My daughter happens to be going steady with the colonel's lieutenant.

Sergeant Steady on.

To Mother Courage: What's your problem with army life, his own father was a soldier wasn't he? Died for his country didn't you tell me?

Mother Courage He's just a wean. You'll lead him by the nose to get slaughtered. Then you'll be off to collect your pieces of silver for him.

Recruiting Officer *To Eilif:* Great base, terrific facilties. Calflength boots you'll never find in civvy street.

Eilif I wouldn't find them from you either.

Mother Courage Aye. Come into my parlour said the spider to the fly.

To Swiss Cheese: Away and raise ructions about this pair trying to lift your brother.

She draws a knife.

Come on you two. Just try it. I'll have the pair of you. We're just quiet folk about our ain business! Ham, claes, that's aw the sort of stuff we're bothered wi. Peaceful people!

Sergeant Very peaceful with that knife in your hand. You ought to be ashamed of yourself. Come on, hand it over. You're just a parasite, living off the fighting. Living off the war, that's all you do. How can you expect to have a war with no soldiers?

Mother Courage They soldiers don't have to be my sons.

Sergeant Oh that's it is it. Happy to take the fruits but not so keen to plant the fruit-trees. Happy to feed off the war but the war's to be starved of any help from you. Call yourself Mother Courage. And you haven't even the stomach for the war that feeds you. Your sons aren't afraid of a fight though, that's for sure.

Eilif I'm up for a fight any day.

Sergeant That's the stuff. Look at me. A soldier since I was seventeen years of age. Not a bad specimen of life, eh?

Mother Courage Your life's no reached three score and ten yet though, has it? That it has not.

Sergeant I'll get there.

Mother Courage Aye. In a box.

Sergeant Trying to put the wind up me are we? You insinuating I've not a full life ahead of me?

Mother Courage Maybe you haveny. Maybe I can tell these things. Maybe I can see you've the sign on you.

Swiss Cheese Mum can tell the future. She's well known.

Recruiting Officer Let her tell your fortune. Give us a laugh.

Sergeant That stuff's all a load of rubbish.

Mother Courage See's your helmet.

The Sergeant gives her his helmet.

Sergeant Total shite. Show us your turn then.

Mother Courage *Takes a sheet of parchment and starts tearing it in bits.* Eilif... Swiss Cheese... Kattrin... The war's goany tear us to bits if we ever get involved in it.

To the Sergeant: Seeing I like you, you can have this fortune for nothing. Look. Death = black. The cross.

Swiss Cheese The other one's got nothing on it, see?

Mother Courage I fold these two pieces of paper, and I put them in your helmet. I give them a good shake, the way we're all shook about the second we're born. Choose!

The Sergeant hesitates.

Recruiting Office *To Eilif* I don't just take anybody you know, I'm very picky. But you've fire in your belly. I like that in a man.

Sergeant *Fishing around in his helmet:* Garbage this whole rigmarole. More sense in a hankie of snot.

Swiss Cheese The black cross! He's a dead man!

Recruiting Officer Don't let them get to you Sergeant. The bullet's not been made that's got your name on it.

Sergeant You conned me there.

Mother Courage Conned yourself the day you signed up for the army. We'd better away and get on with our trade. There's a war on you know.

Sergeant Bloody hell if you think you're beating it you've another think coming. That son of yours is coming with us.

Eilif Good stuff.

Mother Courage Wheesht eejit.

Eilif Swiss Cheese fancies it as well.

Mother Courage I didny foresee that one. Seems like I'll need
to let the three of you see what the future holds.

She goes to the back to draw more crosses on paper

Recruiting Officer *To Eilif:* Ignore any stuff you might've heard
about our lads being a bunch of holy rollers. That sort of
jibe upsets us quite a bit. You maybe have one verse of
a hymn to sing each Sunday, and that's just if you're any
good at singing.

Mother Courage *Returns with the slips and puts them in the
sergeant's helmet.*

Leave their own mother would they the articles, lap up
war like cats wi a bowl a milk indeed. I'll show them what's
what in these bits a paper, they'll see clear enough there's
nay land of milk and honey at the back of this 'Sign up and
you'll rise through the ranks' carry on. I'm scared for my
boys Sergeant, I'm feart they'd never see the end of that
war of yours. There's some gey worrying points a character
in the three of them so there is.

She holds the helmet out to Eilif.

Pick.

*Eilif fishes in the helmet, unfolds a slip. She snatches it from
him.*

There you go. A cross. Does a mother no have enough sor-
rows to bear? He'll die. My own boy to lay doon his life
afore his time. That's the way of it if he joins up. Just like
his father, too much of the bravery about him. If he doesny

see sense he'll be goin the way of aw flesh that bit of paper makes that clear enough. Are you no able to use your loaf for once?

Eilif How do I not?

Mother Courage Cause you'd want to stay by your own mother if you did. And if people called you Chicken you'd just laugh in their face.

Recruiting Officer Shiting it eh. Maybe your brother has more balls.

Mother Courage Laugh in his face. Gawn. Just laugh at him. Here Swiss Cheese your shot. I've less to fear wi you, you're honest.

He fishes in the helmet.

Oh heaven help us, what's that look for? Surely it's blank. Canny be another cross. It canny be I'm to lose you as well. *She takes the slip.* Are you that simple? Swiss Cheese, you'll be done for as well if you don't hawd on to that honesty of yours. That's the way I've reared you, That's for why I always got you to bring the change back from the shops. The only way you'll survive in life. Sergeant, see that. A cross.

Sergeant I can't figure how I got one either. You'll never get me near the front line.

To the Recruiting Officer: Can't be a trick though her children are getting them as well.

Swiss Cheese I'm not accepting mine. Not on your nelly.

Mother Courage *To Kattrin:* Now it's just you Kattrin, you're such a cross yourself with that good heart a yours.

She holds the helmet up high towards the wagon but takes the slip out herself.

I canny take any more a this. Must be a mistake, they canny've been shuffled right. You never mind bein so good-hearted Kattrin you've got a cross in your path as well. Just stay quiet oot the road that shouldny be hard you're dumb in any case. Well that's aw your fortunes told so you're aw goany huv tay watch oot for yourselves. Now let's get back on this wagon and on our way.

She returns the helmet to the sergeant and climbs on the wagon.

Recruiting Officer *To the Sergeant:* Do something about this.

Sergeant I'm feeling a bit queasy.

Recruiting Officer You've maybe picked up a chill having your helmet off in that wind. Try to get her involved in a sale. That beltbuckle Sergeant, how about having a look at it, these people are selling this stuff aren't they? Hey there, the Sergeant's interested in this buckle you've got here.

Mother Courage That's five. And worth four times that. *She clambers down from the wagon*

Sergeant Its secondhand though. A bit windy here. I'll go behind the wagon and have a proper look at it.

He does so.

Mother Courage I don't feel any wind.

Sergeant Maybe it is worth five. There's a bit of silver on it.

Mother Courage *Following him behind the wagon.* A bit? Six solid ounces!

Recruiting Officer *To Eilif:* How about us men going for a drink then. I'll stand the rounds. Let's head.

Eilif stands undecided.

Mother Courage Five it is.

Sergeant I can't get my head round it. I always make sure I'm as far behind the front line as it's possible to be. No safer place during a battle for a sergeant to place himself. Send the rest up the line for their glory, bon bloody voyage. That's the hunger right off me now. I won't be able to swallow a bite.

Mother Courage Never you mind dear, food isn't everything. Just you stay at the back of everythin out of harm's way. Drink. Have a slug.

She gives him a drink.

Recruiting Officer *Who has taken Eilif by the arm and is making off:* A hundred up front and that's you: a soldier of the crown, a fine specimen of manhood and the women will go daft for you. And you can give me one in the eye for insulting you back there.

Both leave. Dumb Kattrin jumps down from the wagon and makes harsh cries.

Mother Courage Right Kattrin, that's us. The Sergeant's paid up! *She holds the banknotes up to the light.* I don't trust any money any more I've been done that often in the past Sergeant. This one seems allright though. We'll be on our way. Where's Eilif?

Swiss Cheese He went away with the recruiting officer.

Mother Courage *Stands quite still, then:* You complete numpty. What are you?

To Kattrin: You *canny* speak I know that. *You're* no to blame.

Sergeant This is reality you're having to face up to now Mother Courage. Have a slug yourself. There's worse ways of living than soldiering. You'd rather live off the war but keep you and yours out of it eh?

Mother Courage You'll to have to help your brother now Kattrin.

Brother and sister get into harness together and pull the wagon. Mother Courage walks at their side.

Sergeant When it's the war that feeds you
It's the war that needs you.

Scene Two

Two years later. Commander's tent. Beside it, a kitchen with Mother Courage and the cook.

The Cook Six for that poxy little chicken!

Mother Courage Poxy little chicken? Poxy little chicken? That's the fattest fowl you'd see in a shop! No way I shouldny get six! That commander of yours would eat a horse for breakfast, it'll be hell on earth for you if there isn't a bite in the kitchen for him.

The Cook You'd pay just one for that off any barrow in the road.

Mother Courage Chickens on barrows in the road? With folk under siege and going about like skeletons? Maybe you can find a rat to feed him with instead. I say maybe, we're nearly out of them as well. Did you not see the men all charging around after a skinny wee rat earlier? OK, seeing it's a siege. Five.

The Cook It's the other side that's under siege. It's us that's doing the besieging. When are you going to get that right?

Mother Courage That's neither here nor there, it's us have got nothing to eat. From what I know the townfolk got loaded up before we hemmed them in. They're happily guzzling and filling their faces to their hearts content. It's us out here have the problem. And the farmers and peasants roundabout haven't got a thing.

The Cook Yes they have. They just keep it out our sight.

Mother Courage No they don't. They haveny a thing to eat. Starvin. They'll dig up roots to eat. Their mouths would be watering if I boiled up that leather belt of yours. That's the way that things are round here. And you think I should give you this chicken for four!

The Cook Three. Not four. Three I said.

Mother Courage This is no ordinary chicken. This is one very special fowl. It used to have music along with its feeding. Had its own favourite march. Bird-brained this bird was not. It could count as well, would you credit that? And you think four's too much for it! I'm tellin you if you don't get something on a plate for that commander of yours soon it's that big fat head of yours he'll have on it.

The Cook End of story. *Takes a slice of beef and starts preparing it.* I'm getting on with this beef. Your last chance.

Mother Courage That meat's well past it. Looks about a year old.

The Cook A *day* old. Yesterday it was mooing in the field.

Mother Courage What a pong. It must have farted before it died.

The Cook I'll get it tender if I have to braise it five hours.

Mother Courage Better smother it in pepper or you'll never hide that stink.

The Commander, the Chaplain and Eilif enter.

The Commander *Slapping Eilif on shoulder.* In you come my son sit yourself down! Sitteth at my right hand O hero of the hour! Thou fought the good fight, vanquished the foes of the Lord in their iniquity! A gold bracelet's in it for you that's for definite – I'll make sure of that once we get our hands on that town. We come all this way to lead the infidel rabble into God's true light and all they do is take their cattle into town where we can't get eating it. The priests'll have so much beef they'll be stuffing it up their arse and down their throats – but you showed them Eilif, you socked it to them. Here's to you my lad, let's see you quaffing some of this fine old red biddy with your own Commander. Holy Wullie there can fuck off. What do you fancy to eat?

Eilif A slice of meat would be nice.

The Commander Hoi there! Cook! Some meat please!

The Cook That's just great. Nothing to eat and he brings guests in for dinner.

Mother Courage makes him stop talking; she wants to listen.

Eilif Takes it out you, killing peasants. You work up an appetite. Mother Courage Mother of God, it's Eilif!

The Cook Who?

Mother Courage My oldest. It's been two years, they snatched him away from me in broad daylight. They high heidyins must have some opinion of him if he's sitting down for his dinner with the Commander! And what have you got for them? Bugger all that's what you have. And the Commander demanding meat. Listen to me cook, you better buy this chicken for the table. Ten it will cost you.

The Commander *Sat down with the Chaplain and Eilif.* Where's the dinner buggerlugs? Let's see it or I'll have your guts for garters!

The Cook Stop blackmailing me, hand over the damn thing.

Mother Courage A 'poxy little chicken' like this?

The Cook For sure. It's not worth five, even that'd be out of order.

Mother Courage Ten I said. Nothing's too expensive for my Eilif, your Commander's blue-eyed boy.

The Cook *Giving her the money.* You can at least pluck it while I get the cooker going.

Mother Courage *Sitting down to pluck the chicken.* Wait till he sees his mother. My own brave, brainy boy. His brother's too simple but at least he's honest. My daughter's nothin. Never utters a word. I suppose at least for that we might be grateful.

The Commander Get that down you lad, my best vintage. Only two cases left, but worth cracking open to meet a Christian soldier at last that still believes in the risen Christ. Our good shepherd over there doesn't know his arse from his elbow let alone his flock. Fill us in Eilif, how did you bring it off? Rubbing out your country bumpkins, making off with twenty of their cattle. Wonderful. The beasts'll be here soon I hope.

Eilif Tomorrow. Day after at the most.

Mother Courage Thank you Eilif. If they were here the day they'd have no need of this chicken.

Eilif This was how I did it. The peasants had sneaked the cattle into the woods under cover of darkness. There were people from the town supposed to come and pick them up. Well I just let them go ahead, rather them than me have the bother of rounding them up, says I to myself. Meantime I made sure our rations started to run out. They were in short enough supply to begin with but I made sure they got shorter. The men were going off their heads for a bit of

meat for their stomachs, they'd start slavering at the very
sound 'm' at the beginning of the word – even if you said
'mmmother!'

The Commander You've really got your head screwed on.

Eilif You're telling me. The rest was no bother. Outnumbered
us three to one they did. Made their attack, things looking
bleak. Four of them corner me under some trees, knock
my weapon out my hand. Game's up I thought. This is it.

The Commander What did you do?

Eilif Laughed.

The Commander You *what?*

Eilif Laughed. Look I said Two hundred a cow's too much let's
make it a hundred and fifty. Hit the ground trading. That
stopped them. What's this guy on about? Quick as you like
I grabbed back my weapon and laid them out cold. Caput.
The mother of invention's necessity, so they say.

The Commander What's your take on that saying, O Watchman of the Night?

The Chaplain It's not Bible-based to be strictly precise on that
point. Though Jesus did turn five loaves into five hundred
to get himself out of another pickle. And he told us to love
one other which is always easier to do when we've all had
something to eat. It's not so easy in the current circum-
stances.

The Commander *Laughing.* Not so easy right enough. Have a
little wine for that pearl of wisdom. Pharisee!
To Eilif: You laid them out cold in the service of the Lord,
Eilif, our lads were hungry and you gave them to eat. What
is it the good book says, 'Whatsoever thou doest unto these
my children, thou doest unto me.' And what did you do

for these our children young fellow-me-lad? You served them up the best steaks-to-be. None of your mouldy loaf, none of your bread and drink out the tin before going into the fight for God's glory.

Eilif Grabbed my weapon and I laid them out cold.

The Commander Like listening to a young Caesar. You must be presented to his majesty.

Eilif I've seen the king from a distance. Seems to cast a kind of light all around his person. I want to be like that.

The Commander You're on your way there lad. You've no idea Eilif how much bravery in a soldier counts with me. Makes me see that fellow as my own flesh and blood.

He takes him to a map. See here Eilif, our strategic position is not very good. There's lots of glory still to be won in the improving of that.

Mother Courage *Who has been listening and is now plucking angrily at the chicken.* That Commander's rubbish.

The Cook Greedy – but why the 'rubbish'?

Mother Courage He says he wants his soldiers brave. Why should he want that? What do you need bravery for if you've planned things right? Whenever I hear people going on about 'soldierly virtues' I know somebody's messed up somewhere.

The Commander What you mean is you know someone's excelled themselves.

Mother Courage I meant what I said. When a king or a general's an eejit and sends his men straight into a trap laid by the other side, that's when you hear them braying on about 'courage'. If they can't find it in their wallets to pay for enough fighting men, that's when they'll rant on about the need to be brave as lions. So-called soldierly virtues– you can stuff them. When you get leaders idle buggers who don't give a toss for working out the overall picture of a situation, it's the men have to suss out what's going on in the battlefield, it's the men who have to show what they call 'presence of mind'; or they're all dead. And loyalty, that's another one they fling in your face. They need it by the bucketful since they're always asking the men to do stuff would make them want to run away. Loyalty, courage, 'presence of mind', all these 'soldierly virtues' a general or a king in any decently run country wouldn't either want or need. A decently run country doesn't need soldierly virtues. Everybody can be just ordinary run of the mill folk, they can be as cowardly as they like if you ask me.

The Commander Your father was a soldier I'll bet.

Eilif They say he was a great soldier. My mum warned me about taking after him. I know a ballad about that.

The Commander On you go. Where's that dinner!

Eilif It's called 'The Ballad of The Wifie and the Sojer'.

He performs a military dance:

> 'The guns they may roar and the bayonets may clash
> but that river will freeze you if in it you dash
> stay away from that ice, take heed my advice'
> said the wifie to the sojer.

> But the sojer just counted his bullets and laughed
> the wardrum was music, thoughts of death were just daft.
> 'I will march to the north and the south wi ma gun
> and ma bayonet in hand through the enemy run'
> said the sojer to the wifie.

'Ach, you'll regret you did not to yir elders give ear
if you spurn the advice that I'm givin you here
stay here on dry land, there's great danger at hand,'
said the wifie to the sojer.

But the sojer with bayonet and bullets on board
threw her words in her face and stepped deep in that ford
sayin water though cold is but harmless;
'When white the moon shines those tiled roofs over there
I'll be back at your side, keep that thought in your prayer'
said the sojer to the wifie.

Mother Courage *Taking up the song from the kitchen and beating time with a spoon:*

Disappeart in a puff! An gone cauld right enough!
nay warmth tay be got frae such doin's!
'Disappeart like the breeze, God help us aw please…'
said the wifie in mind a that sojer.

Eilif What's that?

Mother Courage An the sojer wi bayonet and bullets on board
waded oot in such water as swallowed him up
he sank doon, bayonet up, swept away in yon ford;

and the moon on the tiled roofs it shone cawld an white
but the sojer wi ice was whirled fawr oot a sight
nay words *noo* frae yon sojer tae wifie…

Disappeart in a puff! Gawn cauld right enough!
An she'll never get warmth fray *his* doin's.
'Ach, you'll regret you did not to your elders give ear'
Says the wifie in mind of the soldier.

The Commander Catering staff. They're all the same.

Eilif *Has entered the kitchen and embraced his mother.* Great to
see you mum. Where's the others?

Mother Courage *In his arms.* Happy as pigs in shite. Swiss Cheese got a job as a regiment paymaster so at least he's out the worst of it. I couldn't keep him out the army altogether.

Eilif How's the feet?

Mother Courage I've a devil of a job getting them into my shoes in the morning.

The Commander *Who has come over.* So you're his mother are you. You can provide us with sons like this any time.

Eilf Lucky me, eh? You sitting by in the kitchen hearing me praised to the heavens.

Mother Courage Aye, I heard right enough. *She gives him a box on the ear.*

Eilif Is this for me taking those cattle?

Mother Courage No. It's for no doing the proper thing and givin yourself up when those four had you at their mercy. What have I advised you about looking first after Number One? You're one hell of a wean.

The commander and the Chaplain stand laughing.

Scene Three

Three years later. Military camp, flagpole with regimental flag. Kattrin and mother courage folding washing on a large gun which has a washing line stretched from it to the wagon. Mother Courage bargaining with an officer over a sack of bullets, Swiss cheese in paymaster's uniform looking on.

Pretty Yvette sews a brightly coloured hat with a glass of brandy in front of her. She is in stockinged feet with red highheeled boots beside.

The Officer I'm prepared to sell you these bullets at twenty, which is bargain basement price. Outstanding bargain it is. I need some ready dosh straight off, the Colonel's been hurling it back with the officers for three days and we're running out of booze.

Mother Courage That's Army Issue. If they find them on my wagon I'll be up for court martial. You lot flog off your bullets then send your men into battle with nothing in their rifles.

The Officer Come off it. This is a good deal.

Mother Courage No way I'm taking Army Issue. Not at twenty.

The Officer Sure you can sell them on to Ordinance at Four Regiment for fifty, maybe eighty. Their ordinance officer hasn't got a bullet in his store. Give him a receipt for a hundred and twenty that'll bring him on board.

Mother Courage What's to stop you doing that yourself?

The Officer I know the Ordinance Officer there. I don't trust him. We're pals.

Mother Courage *Takes the bag of bullets.* Let's have it then.

To Kattrin: Away and give him fifteen.

As the officer protests: I said fifteen!

Kattrin drags the bag away. The officer follows.

Mother Courage speaks to Swiss Cheese: Here's your long johns back, you look after those. Here we are in October and autumn on us. Mind you that's not guaranteed the one thing you can be sure of is you can't be sure of anything. Not even the seasons. Those accounts of yours will have to square up proper now that you're regiment paymaster. Have you them squared up all right?

Swiss Cheese Yes Mum.

Mother Courage Never you forget they made you paymaster since you're that honest and you lack your brother's daring it wouldny cross your mind to beat it with the cash. And don't lose those long johns.

Swiss Cheese No Mum, I'll keep them under my mattress. *Begins to leave.*

The Officer Paymaster, I'll come with you.

Mother Courage And never you mind teaching him your shenanigans.

The Officer and Swiss Cheese exit without farewells.

Yvette *Waving:* You might at least say Cheerio officer!

Mother Courage *To Yvette:* A bad article that yin. I don't like seeing him going about with my Swiss Cheese. Mind you the war's not been so very bad to us so far. And afore we know it another four or five years'll have gone and there should be a few more countries involved. So long as I keep my wits about me and my nose clean we should do alright businesswise. You shouldn't be drinking alcohol at this time of the morning, you're not a virtuous woman.

Yvette That's slander I'm not virtuous. Who says?

Mother Courage The dogs in the street are saying it.

Yvette Everybody's badmouthing me, it's driving me up the wall. They steer clear of me in the street as if I was stinkin like some rotten fish. What am I doing this hat up for.

She throws it down.

That's why I need a drink first thing. I never used to do that it gives you bags under your eyes. What's the difference these days. Every squaddie knows me well enough, I should have stayed home with my door shut after that first man of mine did the dirty on me. You can't afford pride in our trade, you just swallow shit or you're out of a job.

Mother Courage Spare us all about you and that Peter of yours again – least not in front of this innocent daughter of mine.

Yvette She's the very one should get it straight from the horse's mouth. Teach her to guard against falling in love.

Mother Courage Naibuddy can guard against that.

Yvette I'll just give the drift of it, get it off my chest. Flanders fields was where I grew up where if I hadn't clapped eyes on Peter I wouldn't be sitting here today. A cook in the army he was. Blonde, Dutch, a bit skinny with it. Watch out for the thin ones Kattrin, they seem to be the worst. I wasn't to know that then, I wasn't to know he already had one girl on the side and she called him Pete the Pipe. Never took his pipe out his mouth when he was making love to her, that was as much as it meant to him.

She sings the Song of Fraternisation:

When I was a lass aged seventeen
an enemy soldier he seemed quite keen
he down to the ground let his sabre land
and with such loving looks did take my hand

    and after the mayday bright
    when there came the mayday night
    the regiment presented arms
    the drums banged out the old alarms
    that soldier took me behind a bush
    and we fraternised.

an affair like this you think you'd puke
that soldier mine, he was a cook
I shunned the sight of him by day
but then at night as one we had our way.

    For after the mayday bright
    there comes the mayday night
    the regiment presents its arms
    the drums bang out the old alarms
    that soldier he takes me behind a bush
    and we come to fraternise.

Such love comes down from heaven above
this ardent passion, this power of love
my friends they can't believe their eyes
how much I love him, him I don't despise

    but then came an awful morn
    bereft it left me, forlorn
    the regiment presented arms
    the drums banged out the old alarms
    that soldier who'd been my lover sweet
    he marched away to the drummers beat.

I was daft enough to chase after him, but it was no use. That's ten years ago.

With swaying gait she goes behind the wagon.

Mother Courage Your hat!

Yvette Whoever wants it it's theres.

Mother Courage That'll learn you Kattrin. Never fling your hat at a soldier. Love is a many splendoured thing that's newly sprung in June, don't you forget it. But it's a path that never runs smooth. A man'll throw himself at your feet – have you washed they feet while we're on the subject – then afore you know where you are you're hooked and chained to the brute for the rest of your natural. You just thank your lucky stars you canny speak. You'll never be caught saying one thing one minute and its opposite the next. You'll never want to bite the tongue out your head cause you've spoke out of turn and told the truth for once. No being able to talk is a great gift from God. Here's the commander's cook. What's *he* looking for.

The cook and Chaplain enter.

The Chaplain I've a message from your son Eilif. Cook's come with me, I think he's taken a shine to you.

The Cook I thought I'd just get a breath of air.

Mother Courage You can have all the air you want if you just keep your hands to yourself. If you don't I'll soon sort you out. What does Eilif want? I've no spare money if that's what he's after.

The Chaplain It's his brother he wants, the paymaster.

Mother Courage He's no here and you'll not get him anywhere else either. He's not Eilif 's paymaster, I'm not for letting that notion get into his head. Eilif can go cadge off somebody else.

She takes money from the purse at her belt.

Here. A sin that's what it is, speculating on mother love. Should be ashamed of himself.

The Cook Hardly. He's off with his regiment straight to his death for all you know. Do you not think he deserves a better sub than that? You women are so tight with the money then you regret it when it's too late.The price of a drink's too much to ask then a bloke's six feet under and you never get the chance to clap eyes on him again.

The Chaplain A long thought, my dear cook, a long thought. But this is no ordinary conflict. Our dead are no misfortuned warriors but indeed they are the bléssed ones. This is a religious war, fought for the true faith and therefore pleasing before God.

The Cook Sure enough it must be a war, what with all the thieving corruption laying waste not to mention a bit of rape going on – but at least it's none of your run of the mill secular wars, this is a holy one! I get the picture. Still even a holy war gives you a thirst.

The Chaplain *To Mother Courage,* pointing to the cook: I tried to keep him away but he says you've cast your spell on him. He sees you in his dreams.

The Cook *Putting a pipe in his mouth:* Drink poured by the hand of lovely woman would be just the job. I'm a bit embarrassed though, there's been a lot of smutty talk on the way here from this Chaplain.

Mother Courage And him a man of the cloth. I'd better see to a drink for the pair of you or you'll no doubt pass the time making improper advances on my modesty.

The Chaplain A tempting woman, the court parson said, falling right way into temptation! *Turning towards Kattrin as he walks:* And who is this enchanting young personage?

Mother Courage That's no an enchanting personage that is a respectable young woman.

The Chaplain and the cook go with Mother Courage behind the cart. While they can be heard conversing Kattrin looks after them then goes and picks up the hat and sits down, pulling the red boots toward her.

Mother Courage The trouble with Poland here is the Poles insisting on sticking their noses in things. Ok so the King made his incursion with the usual military transport, troops what have you, but the Poles couldn't just keep to themselves then could they? No, just when the king's talking of a peaceful withdrawal they go on the attack! They broke the peace. Deserve everything they get so they do.

The Chaplain Spread freedom, that's all his majesty wanted to do. The Poles and Germans were under the yoke of the one Kaiser. They *had* to have freedom brought to them.

The Cook Exactly. Here's to you! Excellent brandy this. I can always tell by somebody's face if they keep good brandy.

Kattrin pulling on the red boots.

And it is a war of religion!

Mind you a hell of an expensive business this 'spreading freedom' isn't it just? And the poorer citizens so unpatriotic the way they complain about having to foot the bill. His majesty locks up the enemy up, removes a few heads from shoulders – and *still* he doesn't win their hearts and minds! At the end of the day, if there weren't so many peoples in the world thirsting for liberty, where on earth could the government go for its military adventures? His majesty invades one country to free folk from evil rule and when that's whetted his moral tastebuds he thinks he'd maybe better just go and free another while he's at it. That country then puts up a pretty good scrap so there isn't much in the way of spoils of war there. So he just has to raise more taxes at home to pay for all the good work done abroad on Johnny Foreigners' behalf. But your narrow- minded ordinary citizen doesn't like dipping all the time into his pocket to pay for foreign wars. Still, governments do have to make 'difficult decisions' don't they, what is it 'hard choices have to be made'? One thing I grant his majesty. He did it all on his basis of a sincere Christian faith. If you didn't know that you might think he was just in it to feather his own nest. He made every move with a trouble-free conscience. Butter wouldn't melt in his mouth. You have to hand it to him.

Mother Courage You're not one of his subjects or you'd be more careful the way you speak about the conquering hero.

The Chaplain It's him puts the bread in your mouth.

The Cook I don't eat the stuff. I only bake it.

Mother Courage He'll never lose. His soldiers just swallow all that stuff he comes away with. *seriously* To listen to the folk at the top you'd think we were fighting for God and 'sacred principles' and all that carry on. Underneath they're no *that* daft, they're in it for what they can get. And that's what keeps small fry like us involved as well. If it wasny for that we wouldny give them the time of day.

The Cook Spot on.

The Chaplain I think you should take note of the flag here when you're so free with your opinions.

Mother Courage Protestants and proud!

The Cook Cheers!

Kattrin struts about with Yvette's hat on. Suddenly cannon and shots. Mother Courage the cook and the Chaplain rush to the front of the cart, glasses in hand. The Ordinance Officer and a soldier run to the cannon and try to push it along.

Mother Courage What's going on. Let me get my washing there.

She tries to rescue her washing.

The Officer Catholics! They're all over the place! We might not get out of this.

To the Soldier: Move that gun!

He runs off.

The Cook God almighty I need to find the commander. See you in a couple of days, we can carry on this conversation then.

He rushes off.

Mother Courage Your pipe!

The Cook You hold on to it I'll be needing it!

Mouther Courage This had to happen just as I'm making some money.

The Chaplain I think I had better be on my way too. It's a little dangerous here with the enemy upon us. Blessed are the peacemakers, those are fine words in a war. I could do with a coat to hide my attire.

Mother Courage You're getting no coat from me. Not to save your skin either, I've had bother with coats like that before.

The Chaplain I'm a walking target, I've got 'Protestant' written all over me!

Mother Courage Here.

Brings him a coat.

Against my better judgement. Now vamoose.

The Chaplain Thank you indeed your generosity of spirit commends you. But I'll just sit where I am, running would only draw attention to me.

Mother Courage *To the Soldier:* Leave it, you're not getting paid to do that! That'll cost you your life, let me see to it.

The Soldier *Running away:* You're my witness. I did try.

Mother Courage Never mind I'll swear to it. *Seeing Kattrin with the hat:* What are you at with that whore's hat? Get it off you. Are you off your head? – the Catholics are coming.

She tears the hat off her head.

Do you want them to think you're on the game? And the fuck me boots! I'll get them off her.

She tries to get them off.

Holy God Chaplain give us a hand with these boots. I'll be right back.

She runs to the wagon.

Yvette *Entering powdering her face.* The Catholics are coming. Where's my hat? Who's been messing it about? I'd look a right sight in that, they'd have some opinion of me. I've no mirror either.
To the Chaplain: How's my face? Is this too much powder?

The Chaplain Eh... just the job.

Yvette The boots. My red boots.

She can't find them because Kattrin is hiding her feet under her skirt.

I left them in this place. Now I'll need to go back to my tent in my bare feet. It's a disgrace.

Swiss Cheese comes running in carrying the cash box.

Mother Courage *Enters with her hands covered with ashes.*

To Kattrin: Ashes! Quick!

To Swiss Cheese: What's that you've there?

Swiss Cheese The regiment's cash box.

Mother Courage Get rid of it! You're finished with that paymaster job.

Swiss Cheese It's my duty! *He goes to the back.*

Mother Courage *To the Chaplain:* And you get that minister's collar off you or they'll see you for what you are coat or no coat.

Rubbing ashes into Kattrin's face: Hold your face still, this'll be the saving of you. This is a disaster, the sentries must

have been drunk. Come on then just hide your light under a bushel that's what we're enjoined. All a squaddie needs is to see a woman with a clean face and that's her on her back. Specially a Catholic squaddie. Starved for weeks then they're let loose on any women they can find. That'll do you fine. Look like you've been up to the eyes in glaur. Stop you're chittering you should be safe now.
To Swiss Cheese: Where did you dump that cash box?

Swiss Cheese I decided just to hide it in the wagon.

Mother Courage *Horrified.* The wagon! In the name of God what kind of numpty are you? I turn my back for a minute and you've got the three of us likely to be hung!

Swiss Cheese OK I'll plank it somewhere else. Or go away with it.

Mother Courage Stay. It's too late for that.

The Chaplain *Still changing his clothes.* Heavens above. The flag!

Mother Courage *Hauling down the flag.* Christ almighty I never notice this bloody thing any more. I've had it that long. Twenty five year.

The sound of cannon grows.

Three days later. Morning. The cannon is gone. Mother Courage, Kattrin, the Chaplain and Swiss Cheese sit eating.

Swiss Cheese Three whole days stuck here on my backside. The sergeant's sure to be saying to himself, 'where's Swiss Cheese with that cash box?'

Mother Courage Relax. They've no notion where you are.

The Chaplain What about my position of pastoral care? I can't hold a prayer meeting. I'd be done for. Scripture says 'Out of the abundance of the heart the tongue speaketh.' And I can't give speech!

Mother Courage There you go. The one wi his religion the other wi his cash box. And I'm buggered if I know which is the more likely to get us in trouble.

The Chaplain All of us are in the hands of the Almighty.

Mother Courage Oh I hope it's no as bad as that. I can hardly get a wink a sleep at night as it is. Might be safer for us if you wereny here Swiss Cheese… still. I've managed alright so far. I told them I'm as much against the anti-Christ as anybody else, I'd seen him the big Swede with the horns in his head. The left horn's a bit the worse for wear I told them. When they were spiering all their questions at me I kept asking if they knew where I could lay my hands on some cheap holy candles. I know all about it Swiss Cheese's father was a Catholic, he'd kid on about it. I don't think they fell for my patter mind but they do need a canteen wagon so I think they just never let on. It'll all come out in the wash fine. We're prisoners right enough but so's fleas in a fur coat.

The Chaplain The milk here's very good. But we may have to tighten our belts now. We're on the losing side – defeated.

Mother Courage Who's defeated. Victory and defeat at the top's no the same as at the bottom you know. No way. You get so-called defeats that's victories for us at the bottom of the heap. Maybe some *honour's* lost, but who gives a monkeys for that. There was an occasion once in Livonia, our side was so soundly defeated in a battle it was total chaos. Well that gave me the opportunity to swipe a grey horse out the baggage train. And that horse hauled this cart for seven months. Then in the end we won, the buggers took an inventory and I lost my horse. All the same to us yins at the bottom a the heap who wins or loses. It's us that pay the price at the end of the day. The best thing is when politics just gets stuck.

To Swiss Cheese: Eat that up.

Swiss Cheese Yuch. How's the sergeant going to pay the men now?

Mother Courage You don't get your pay if you're running away.

Swiss Cheese They could go on strike then. Dig their heels in.

No pay, we're not moving.

Mother Courage I worry about they scruples of yours Swiss Cheese. I brought you up honest since you're not the full shilling in the brains department. But don't get carried away with yourself. I'm away with this Chaplain here to get some meat and a Roman Catholic flag. The reverend can track down a bit of meat in his sleep. He can tell how good a cut it is by how much he starts slavering. Good job they let me keep my business. All that matters is how much they pay not what foot they dig with. Protestant trousers keep your legs just as warm as Catholic ones.

The Chaplain As the mendicant monk said when he heard the Lutherans were bringing revolution to the country – 'They'll still require beggars once it's over.'

Mother Courage disappears into the wagon.

She won't keep her mind off that cash box. The Catholics haven't bothered us so far, they must think we're all with the wagon. But I don't see that lasting.

Swiss Cheese I can get *rid* of the box.

The Chaplain Doing so could be be even more dangerous if they saw you going about it. They've spies everywhere.

Yesterday morning I was relieving myself in a hole in the ground and one of them jumped out of it. Gave me such a fright I almost broke into prayer, that would have done for me. Apparently they think they can tell a Protestant by the aroma from his stool. Dreadful little beast this fellow was, he had a patch over his eye.

Mother Courage *Clambering out of the wagon with a basket.* So this is what you've been up to have you no shame madam?

She holds up Yvette's boots.

Yvette's very boots! Swiped them cool as you like. That was you with your 'enchanting personage' talk.

She lays them in the basket.

Stealing Yvette's boots! She at least makes a spectacle of herself for the money, you'll do it for damn all but the pleasing of your own self. I've told you, this can all wait to peacetime. You're for no soldier, never mind putting on airs and graces for any of them.

The Chaplain She doesn't put on airs and graces.

Mother Courage She can cut her cloth to suit her station. I'm happy enough with her when folk say 'Oh I never noticed that poor lassie of yours'. If they think she's just another pebble on the beach that's fine by me.
To Swiss Cheese: Leave the cash box where it is do you hear me? And look after that sister of yours she can do with some looking after. Pair of you'll be the death of me. I'd have an easier time managing a bag of fleas.

She leaves with the Chaplain. Kattrin clears the dishes away.

Swiss Cheese Not so many days now and it won't be warm enough to go about without a jacket.

Kattrin points to a tree.

Yep, the leaves are turning yellow.

With gestures Kattrin asks if he wants a drink.

Nothing to drink thanks, I'm thinking here. *Pause.*

Can't sleep for thinking about it she says. Maybe I should plank that cash box. I know where it can go, a rat's hole at the river's edge, I could stuff it in there for now and get it back before daybreak. Thanks Kattrin, I will have that drink.

Kattrin goes behind the cart.

Take the cashbox back then to the regiment. They can't have gone very far in three days. Sergeant'll think he's seeing things. 'Swiss Cheese, how nice to have my expectations disappointed. First I trust you with the regimental cash box, then you bring it back!'

When Kattrin reappears with a glass two men confront her. One of them is a sergeant. The other doffs his hat and flourishes it in a showy greeting. He has a bandage over one eye.

Man with Eyepatch Good day miss. Any chance seen a bloke from Protestant Regiment Two hereabouts?

Kattrin runs away, spilling her drink. The two men withdraw after seeing Swiss Cheese sitting.

Swiss Cheese *Starting up from reflection:* You've spillt that drink! What's up can you not look where you're going? I don't know. I'm away I've decided what to do about this.

He stands up. She does all she can to alert him to the danger he is in. He pushes her away.

I don't know what you're on about. I know you mean well but you just can't get it across can you. Never mind about the drink, there's plenty more where that came from.

He takes the cash box out of the wagon and puts it under his coat.

Be right back. Don't try and stop me or I'll have to tell you off. I realise you're doing your best just a shame you can't speak.

When she tries to hold him back he kisses her and pulls himself free. Exit. She is desperate and runs up and down emitting little sounds. Mother Courage and the Chaplain return. Kattrin rushes at her mother.

Mother Courage What's all this carry on? Pull yourself together Kattrin! Has somebody done something? Where's Swiss Cheese?

To Chaplain. Stop hanging about get that Catholic flag up!

She takes a flag out of her basket and the Chaplain runs it up the pole.

The Chaplain *Bitterly.* All devout Roman Catholics now.

Mother Courage Cool down Kattrin tell your mother she can understand. What. So that thrawn bugger a mine's away with the cash box. I'll clatter him the devil. Now just you hold on and take your time never mind trying to talk, just use your hands. I don't like you making they noises like a hound what do you think the Chaplain makes of it. You're giving him the heeby jeebies. Somebody with just one eye was here?

The Chaplain That one-eyed man's an informer. Have they got Swiss Cheese?

Kattrin shakes her head, shrugs her shoulders.

We're done for.

The two men bring in Swiss Cheese.

Swiss Cheese Leave go of me! I've nothing to hide. You'll break my shoulder! I'm totally innocent!

The Sergeant This is where he came from. Those're his friends.

Mother Courage What. Us? Since when?

Swiss Cheese I don't know these folk at all. I just bought my lunch here. You maybe saw me on that bench. It was too salty by the way.

The Sergeant Who exactly are you people?

Mother Courage Ordinary decent law-abiding folk. He did buy his food here, that's correct. And it was too salty.

The Sergeant You trying to say you don't know this man?

Mother Courage I canny know everybody that comes here can I. I don't ask everybody What's your name and are you by any chance one of these infidels? Folk who hand over their money never strike me as infidels. You an infidel?

Swiss Cheese No way.

The Chaplain He sat like one schooled in the ways of right-eousness and showed no inclination to open his mouth. Except to eat of course.

The Sergeant Who are *you* then?

Mother Courage He's just my barman. You'll likely have a drouth on you gentlemen, would you fancy a wee drink? You'll be legweary with all that chasing about.

The Sergeant No alcohol on duty.

To Swiss Cheese. You did have something on you, we saw the bulge under your shirt. You must've hid it somewhere along the river.

Mother Courage Are you sure it's him?

Swiss Cheese It was another bloke. There *was* another guy with a bulge under his shirt, I saw it myself. You've the wrong man.

Mother Courage That's my take on it as well. A mixup, it happens aw the time. I know what folk are like, I'm Mother Courage. You'll have heard all about me, everybody knows who Mother Courage is. I'm telling you, that's an honest boy you've got there, you can see it in his face.

The Sergeant It's the regimental cash box we're trying to track down. We know what the man who had it looks like. That's you.

Swiss Cheese No it isn't!

The Sergeant And if you don't give it back to us you're a dead man, ok? Now where is it.

Mother Courage *Urgently:* Of course the boy would hand it over to save his life wouldn't he now. He would speak and say that's right here's where it is I can tell when I'm beaten. He's not that stupit no to tell you, is he? Speak up daftie he's gien you a chance!

Swiss Cheese And what if I don't have the thing?

The Sergeant We're taking you in. We'll have it out you soon enough. *They take him off.*

Mother Courage Shouting after them: He would own up! He's no that daft! Mind that shoulder of his you'll break it. Runs after them.

The same evening. The Chaplain and Kattrin are cleaning glasses and polishing knives.

The Chaplain The history of religion is replete with the stories of those taken into captivity, just like the case in hand. Witness the Passion of Our Lord and Saviour himself. This tells that story.

It was in the first hour of the day
that Jesus Christ was led away
like common murderer, they say
to Pilate, the heathen judge.

Though he in Christ could find no fault
no sign of treason nor assault
proceedings yet he would not halt
and sent Jesus to Herod.

At three they took Our Lord, God's son
scourged him with whips bare flesh upon
crowned him with painful benison
– a crown of thorns:

clad in mock regal robes of state
smitten with clubs and words of hate
given the cross of mankind's weight
to carry to his death.

At six they stripped our saviour bare
nailed to a cross they hung him there
bleeding from wounds in want of care
he prayed, and gave lamentation.

On his either side two felons hung
who joined in the sneers with mocking tongue
Our Lord hung lone midst jeers among
and the sun left the sky.

At nine in anguish Christ gave cry
my God thou hast forsaken me. Why?
But mocking that now his mouth was dry
they gave him a cup of vinegar.

When Jesus died, all spirit spent
great tremors shook earth's fundament
the sacred temple curtain rent
and many a boulder shattered.

Those thieves at dusk who hung beside
they broke their legs that soon they died
then took a spear to Jesus' side
and plunged it in.

Both blood and water poured from thence
scorned him they yet without penitence
this son of man, whose recompense
was to save humanity.

Mother Courage *Entering excitedly.* It's life or death for oor Swiss Cheese now. The sergeant's still persuadable so long as he doesny know Swiss Cheese is family or he'll say we're behind the whole thing. He'll need his palms greased with money, but where can we lay our hands on enough at this stage? Was Yvette no here a wee while ago? I bumped into her on the way over she'd a colonel in tow. Maybe he'd like to buy a canteen wagon for her!

The Chaplain You would sell the wagon and all your worldly goods?

Mother Courage Where else will I get the money to buy off the sergeant?

The Chaplain And how would you get by once that was gone?

Mother Courage That's a big question.

Enter Yvette with an old colonel.

Yvette *Embracing Mother:* Courage Darling Mrs Courage, fancy meeting you again! *Whispering:* He's up for it! Aloud: This is my friend whom I ehm consult on matters of business. I couldn't help overhearing you say you would like to sell this wagon of yours. It just so happens I might like to consider purchasing it myself.

Mother Courage I wouldny sell it straight out, I'm just for pawning it, leasing it a wee while then buying it back. I'm no sellin it outright. You'll no get many wagons as good as that one during a war.

Yvette *Pawn* it? I thought it was an outright sale you were talking about. I don't know I'm all that interested now. *To the colonel:* What do you think dearest?

The Colonel Your wish is my command.

Mother Courage Only a pawn.

Yvette I thought you said you *had* to have the cash.

Mother Courage *Firmly:* That's right. But I'll definitely make sure I pawn it rather than sell it for good. That's our living that cart. This is still a chance for you though to make some money. You don't know when another wagon is going to turn up. Or when you'll pick up another man to ehm, advise you on your business matters.

The Colonel Just take the wagon.

Yvette My friend thinks we should shake on this but I'm not happy it's only for pawn. We should buy it outright that's what you think don't you?

The Colonel Absolutely. Absolutely sweetie.

Mother Courage Then you'll better away try and find one that's for sale. You never know you might be lucky if you've time to spare and your pal goes with you. Maybe in a week or a fortnight you might be lucky.

Yvette I suppose we could shop around for something. I love shopping around, I love sloping around with my Poldy Woldy here…

The Colonel Gosh. Do you really?

Yvette Oh, yes! It's such fun! I could do *that* for a fortnight!

The Colonel Gosh. Could you really?

Yvette If you did get cash for pawning it, when would you prop- ose to redeem the cart with the money?

Mother Courage After a couple a weeks, maybe just the one.

Yvette I don't know what…. Poldi darling, *advise me.*

She takes the colonel to one side.

She'll *have* to let it go, don't worry. I might just get the money from that blonde lieutenant, you know the one, he'll come up with the readies for me. He's nuts about me, says I make him think of someone else. What do you think?

The Colonel You really ought to have nothing to do with that chap, a bad egg altogether, he'd only take advantage of you. I did say *I'd* treat you, didn't I?

Yvette Oh I couldn't possibly let you!

The Colonel Please! This one's on me!

Yvette Well, if you think the lieutenant only wants to take advantage of me…

The Colonel I do think that.

Yvette So you advise me to accept…?

The Colonel Absolutely sweetie. Absolutely.

Yvette *To Mother Courage:* My friend says That'll be fine. Make out a receipt that the wagon becomes mine and everything in it when two weeks are up. I'll just take stock right away and give you two thousand later.

To the Colonel: On you go to camp, I'll be along in a while. I have to check all this stuff to make sure nothing goes missing from *my* wagon later.

She kisses him. He leaves. She climbs up on the cart.

You've hardly got any boots left!

Mother Courage It's no the time now to be going through that wagon no matter whose it is. You said you'd talk to the Sergeant, we've no got a minute to lose, Swiss Cheese's to be court martialled in an hour.

Yvette I want to double check the number of shirts you have here.

Mother Courage *Dragging her by the skirt:* You'd drain the blood out a corpse! Swiss Cheese is facing a death sentence. Don't say where you got the money say it's your fiancé. God struth we'll all be in it for this.

Yvette I've to meet that man with the patch over his eye near the woods. He'll be there now.

The Chaplain I don't think you should give two thousand. Fifteen hundred seems quite enough.

Mother Courage Whose money is this? You mind your own business. You'll have your face shaped for your bowl of food when the time comes no doubt. Away you go and don't haggle with him there's a life at stake here. *Pushes Yvette off.*

The Chaplain I wasn't trying to take over but how are we going to get by? Your daughter's a liability, no chance of *her* finding a job.

Mother Courage I'm banking on that regimental cash box smart arse. That should cover what this whole business is costing us.

The Chaplain Do you think she'll manage to bring it off?

Mother Courage It'll suit her just fine to do so. I hand over the two thousand and she takes possession of the wagon. She knows what side her loaf's buttered on, that colonel won't be dancing to her tune the rest of her life. Kattrin, get some pumice and see to those knives. And you, stop huxterin about like Christ in the garden of Gethsamene. Get they glasses washed out right now. There's fifty cavalry coming by the night and you'll be moaning about having to run after them. 'I'm not obliged to run after folk in the church' you'll no doubt be telling us. I think he'll get the pardon. Thank God they're crooked, they're not like animals, they're just human beings, all they want is some money under the table. The Lord gives and men are on the take, that's the way of the world. Our hope is in backhanders. As long there's backhanders you've compassionate judges and even innocent folk can walk free.

Yvette *Comes panting in.* They've only agreed two thousand if you give them it straight off, but things are changing all the time. I'll get him with the one eye to the colonel right away. Swiss Cheese has owned up he took the cashbox, they put the thumbscrews on him. He flung the box in the river when he saw them coming. That's that gone for good. Will I get the money from the colonel now?

Mother Courage Gone for good? How'll I get my money back?

Yvette Oh that was the plan was it, you'd get your hands on the cashbox and I could forget about inheriting the wagon eh? No way Mother Courage. If you want your Swiss Cheese alive you're going to have to give everything up. Or do I forget the whole thing and you just keep the wagon?

Mother Courage I wasny to see this turnabout. All right, stop your hasslin, you'll get the wagon, your wagon it is, my wagon that's been for the past seventeen year. I need to think about this a minute, it's too much all at once. What can I do? I canny hand over two thousand, I should have tried to beat them down. You need *something* in your pocket or anybody that's just got the notion can shove you in the gutter when they feel like it. Go tell them it's a twelve hundred or nothing. Even at that I've still lost the wagon.

Yvette They won't do it for that. And him with the eyepatch is jittery, he keeps looking over his shoulder he's so wound up. Shouldn't I better give over the whole lot?

Mother Courage *In despair:* I canny pay that! Thirty years I've worked. She's twenty five and still no got a man. I've her future to think about. Let me be. I know what. Twelve hundred or they can forget it.

Yvette It's your call. *She runs off.*

Mother Courage walks slowly to the rear, turns, looking neither at Kattrin nor the Chaplain, sits down to help Kattrin with the knives.

Mother Courage Watch you don't break they glasses they're not ours. And mind or you'll go cutting yourself. Swiss Cheese will be back, they'll get their two thousand if that's what's required. Your brother'll be back. With eight hundred mind you we could pack a hamper with stuff and start on the road again. It wouldn't be the end of the story.

The Chaplain The good book tells us, The Lord will provide.

Mother Courage I told you to dry them properly.

The clean the knives in silence. Suddenly Kattrin runs sobbing behind the wagon.

Yvette *Running in.* They won't accept it, I told you they wouldn't. He was just for forgetting the whole thing on the spot. What's the point he says the drums will be rolling any second for the verdict. I said make it fifteen hundred, he just shrugged. He could hardly be bothered hanging on for me to come back here.

Mother Courage Two thousand. Run!

Yvette runs. Mother Courage sits, silent. The Chaplain has stopped doing the glasses.

I think maybe... I'm feart I've held out too long.

In the distance a roll of drums. The Chaplain stands up and walks towards the rear. Mother Courage remains seated. It grows dark. It gets light again. Mother Courage has not moved.

Yvette *Arrives, pale.* You've done it now. You and your haggling. The wagon's yours now alright. Eleven bullets, that's what he copped. I don't know why I even bother with you, you're not worth it. They don't think the cashbox is in the river by the way. They think it's here, you and he are connected. I think they're bringing the body to see if you give yourself a showing up when you see it. Better control your feelings or we're a goner. They're at my back. Will I keep Kattrin away?

Mother Courage shakes her head.

Does she know what's happening? Maybe she didn't hear the drums or know what they mean.

Mother Courage She knows. Bring her.

Yvette brings Kattrin, who walks over to her mother and stands by her. Mother Courage takes her hand. Two men come on with a stretcher; there is a sheet on it and something underneath. Beside them, the Sergeant. They put the stretcher down.

The Sergeant This is somebody we don't have a name for. We need the name for the records. He'd a meal here have a look at him see if you can tell us who he is.

He pulls back the sheet. Know who he is?

Mother Courage shakes her head.

So, you've never seen him before that meal.

Mother Courage shakes her head.

Pick him up. Throw him in the corpse pit. Nobody knows his name.

Scene Four

Outside an officer's tent. Mother Courage waiting. A clerk sticks his head out.

The Clerk I recognise you. You'd a Protestant paymaster hiding with you. You'd better not complain about anything.

Mother Courage I will so! I've done nothin wrong and you'd think I had if I kept my mouth shut about it. They cut everything to bits in my waggon then fined me five for nothin. Absolutely nothin!

The Clerk If I were you I'd keep quiet. Cause we're short of canteen wagons we let the likes of you carry on, the more so if you've something to hide and need a fine every so often.

Mother Courage I'm puttin in a grievance procedure.

The Clerk So be it. You can wait here till the Captain's free. *He withdraws into the tent.*

A Young Soldier *Storming in:* Fuck that captain! Where is the bastard? He's knocked my prize money to get drink for him and his fancywomen! I'll tear his guts out!

An Older Soldier *Coming after him:* Shut your gob or you'll get lifted.

The Young Soldier Out here, come on ya thieving bastard, I'll kick lumps out you! I'm the one who swam the river and he swans off with the fucking dough! I haven't even the money for a pint. Come on! I'll slice you in bits man.

The Older Soldier Jesus God he'll end up in shit street for this.

The Young Soldier Leave go of me or you'll be the one that gets it. This is for getting sorted right now.

The Older Soldier He saved the colonel's horse and didn't get the reward promised for it. He's just a boy, doesn't know the score in these things.

Mother Courage Leave him. You needny tie him up, he's no a dog. Fair enough that he wants his money. Why else would he cover himself in glory?

The Young Soldier In there knocking it back! The lot of you are chicken. It was me done the heroic stuff, I want the fuckin dough for it!

Mother Courage Never mind bawlin the odds at me, I've no got my ain troubles to seek. I'd watch that voice of yours as well you'll need it when the captain comes. At this rate you'll have shouted yourself speechless an he'll no have the satisfaction of makin an example of you till you drop in a faint. Folk that rant on like yourself never rant long, they're wanting sung to sleep soon enough, they're that tired.

The Young Soldier I'm no tired and to hell with sleep. I'm starving. The stuff they call bread we get here is just acorns and hempseed and no much of that either. While he's in there knocking back my money I'm dying for something to eat. I'll have the bastard.

Mother Courage I get it. You're hungry. Last year it's off the main road and across the fields the Commander orders you, so what happens. The crops are trampled flat. I could have been selling boots marked up at a hundred, if only anybody had had any money, and I'd had any boots. He never thought he'd still be stuck here this year but stuck he is and there's nay food. I get the picture. You've had it up to here.

The Young Soldier Talk all you like, I'm not putting up with injustice.

Mother Courage Fair do's. But how long? How long are you no puttin up wi injustice for? An hour? Couple a hours? Huvny asked yourself that have you. But that's the nub a the matter. Hellish havin to take the punishment, but more so if it's only then you see the injustice.

The Young Soldier I don't know why I have to put up wi your patter. Where's that captain?

Mother Courage You know fine well I'm tellin you the truth. You're losing that anger a yours already. Just a teeny wee rage wasn't it. It's a good long one you need. But how are you going to come up with that?

The Young Soldier Are you saying I shouldn't be demanding this reward?

Mother Courage The opposite. All I'm sayin is your anger willny last. You'll no get anywhere wi it which is a real shame. If you held onto that anger a yours, I'd be with you all the way. I'd say on you go pal, carve him up. What's the point of me doin that though if you just cave cause you've crapped out of it? You just stand there like a stookie while the captain reads the riot act at you.

The Older Soldier That's correct, he's off his head.

The Young Soldier Am I indeed. Watch this. Now you'll see who's going to do the carving.

Draws his weapon.

When he comes here, I'm going to carve him into ribbons.

The Clerk Captain'll be out in a minute.

In the tone of a military command: Sit!

The young soldier sits.

Mother Courage   – and down he sits. What did I say ? Down in a flash. They see right through us. They know how to operate. Sit! And down we sit. The armchair revolutionaries. Never mind getting to your feet, no the same as last time, just sit where you are. You needny feel too ashamed, I'm no any better, not a bit of it. We don't rock the boat do we, it'd be bad for business. Let me tell you the story of the great capitulation.

Sings:

Once in years gone by, in my springtime bloom
I fancied that I'd have it all my own sweet way in time

(I wasny jist yer average woman frae a single end, I had ma looks I was sharp as a tack and I'd ma sights aimed high)

– and I'd not take shit, if my soup contained a hair
right away they had to change the plate or else

(it's absolutely all or nothin, secondbest is not an option, yi get what you fight for, yi huvty make your own rules)

but a burdie tweet my ear
psst! in a year
you'll keep in step like aw the rest
parade in time not be a pest
you'll tootle away yir own wee tune
march up and doon
right turn! yir mates and aw
they'll say it's God's law
an you'll no say a thing.

an afore a year I had failed the test
I'd swallowed doon ma medicine like aw the rest.

(two weans roon ma ankles the price o a loaf skyhigh and aw the rest o it)

I was so done in, jist feelin knackered all the time
them in charge, they had me by the short and curlies

(you have to get by wi other folk, one haun washes the
other yin, it's nay use bangin yir heid against a brick wall)

an a burdie tweet my ear
psst! in a year
she'll keep in step like aw the rest
parade in time not be a pest
she'll tootle away her own wee tune
march up and doon
right turn! her mates and aw
they'll say it's God's law
an she'll no say a thing.

I have seen some folk, the heavens above they'd storm
there's no a star they think too big or jist too faur away

(if you've talent you'll rise, where there's a will there's a
way, anybody can make it to the top)

but I'll tell you this, if you set off up icy mountain peaks
then you'll find a wee straw hat is no inuff

(You have to make out in life wi what you've got)

an a burdie tweet my ear
psst! in a year
we'll keep in step like aw the rest
parade in time no be a pest
we'll tootle away wir own wee tune
march up and doon
right turn! wir mates and aw
they'll say it's God's law
an we'll no say a thing.

to the young soldier So you just keep that weapon out if
you're really up for it and your anger's big enough. You've

every reason, definitely. But if you have just got a wee
anger that willny last – forget it.

The Young Soldier Ach to hell with this. *Exit followed by the
Older Soldier.*

The Clerk *Sticks his head out:*Captain's ready now. He'll hear
your grievance.

Mother Courage I've changed my mind. Nothing's the matter.
Exit.

Scene Five

Three years later. A war-ruined village. The cart by a badly shot-up village. Distant military music. Two soldiers being served by Kattrin and Mother Courage. One of them has a woman's fur coat over his shoulders.

Mother Courage What do you mean you've no money? No money, no drink. They can play their victory marches aw they like, the men are in need a money.

The First Soldier I need a drink! I didn't get there in time for all the looting. That mingy general only had only gave us an hour in the town to grab what we wanted. 'I feel for these people' he says. The townsfolk must have lined his wallet.

The Chaplain *Staggering in.* There's more in the farm house. A whole family. I need a hand. I need linen bandage!

The second soldier goes with him. Kattrin getting very excited. She tries to get her mother to bring linen out.

Mother Courage I don't have any. I sellt all my bandage already to the regiment. And I'm no tearing up officers' shirts for they folk.

The Chaplain *Calling over his shoulder:* I told you I need linen!

Mother Courage *Stoppin Kattrin from entering the wagon:* Not one piece! They've got damn aw and they'll pay damn aw.

The Chaplain *To a woman he is carrying in:*Why did you stay out here when they were attacking?

The Woman Our farm...

Mother Courage Did you think these folk would ever let anythin out their hands? And now I'm supposed to foot the bill! No thank you.

The First Soldier They're Proddies. How come they're Protestants?

Mother Courage Doesny matter to them now what they are. They've lost their farm.

The Second Soldier They're not Protestants in any case. They're Catholic.

The First Soldier You canny sort them out when you're shelling them.

A Peasant *Brought in by the Chaplain:* My arm's away…

The Chaplain Where's that linen?

All look at Mother Courage, who does not budge.

Mother Courage I canny give stuff away for nothin. You just think what I have to pay in income tax, vat, bribes for officials.

Kattrin takes up a board and threatens her mother with it, emitting gurgling sounds.

Have you lost the place? Put that doon or I'll clatter you wi it ya daft bitch. I'm handin over sweet damn all I need it aw myself.

The Chaplain lifts her bodily off the steps of the wagon and sets her down on the ground. He takes out shirts from the wagon and tears them in strips.

Ma shirts! Ma good officers's shirts!

From the house come the cry of a child in pain.

The Peasant My baby's still in there. *Kattrin runs in.*

The Chaplain *To the woman:* Just stay there. She'll get it for you.

Mother Courage Stop her, the roof 'll be comin down on her!

The Chaplain I'm not going back in!

Mother Courage *Pulled in both directions:* Go easy wi my best linen!

The second soldier holds her back. Kattrin brings a baby out of the ruins.

Another wean to haul about, you'll be fair taken on with yourself? Give it this minute to its mother or we'll be hard put to get it off you; took hours the last time. You listenin?

To the second soldier: Never mind stannin gawpin, away and tell them they can cut out the victory music, victory's plain enough for us to see. Aw victory means to me is losing out.

The Chaplain *Bandaging.* The blood's coming through.

Kattrin is rocking the baby and humming a lullaby.

Mother Courage Would you look at that yin, the picture a bliss in aw this mess. Hand that wean back, the mother's comin round. *She sees the first soldier. He had been handling the drinks, and is now trying to make off with the bottle.* Hey steady on buggerlugs. Think the bottle's loot as well do you! You can pay for it!

The First Soldier I've absolutely no money.

Mother Courage *Snatching the fur coat from him:* This coat'll do fine. You knocked it anyway.

The Chaplain There's somebody still in there.

Scene Six

One year later. Inside a canteen tent. The inner side of a counter at the rear. In the distance drums and funeral music. The Chaplain and the regimental clerk are playing draughts. Mother Courage and her daughter are stocktaking.

The Chaplain The funeral cortege is setting off.

Mother Courage Shame the way the general went. Twenty two pairs a socks... Just his hard luck it was so foggy. The fields were thick with it that mornin, that was what was to blame. Your man calls up another regiment tells them to fight till the death then heads back to camp as usual. Only he gets mixed up in the fog and starts going forwards instead of back. Ends up shot in the battlefield. Just four lamps left...

A whistle from the rear. She goes to the counter.

To a soldier: That's terrible the way you lot are skiving off from your own general's funeral!

She pours a drink.

The Clerk They shouldn't have been paid before the funeral. Now they're giving the funeral a miss and just getting drunk.

The Chaplain *To the clerk:* Should you not be at the funeral yourself?

The Clerk I thought I'd stay away seeing as it's raining.

Mother Courage Different for you right enough you'll want to keep your uniform dry. I gather they wanted tolling bells as you'd expect but the general had had them all shot down so the poor soul won't be hearing any bells when he's lowered into his grave. They're goany fire three rifle shots over him so it won't be *too* quiet. Sixteen leather belts….

Voice from Counter Anybody serving here? Brandy!

Mother Courage Let's see your money first. And no, no way you're coming in here with they boots on your feet. You can have your drink outside rain or no rain. Officers Only in here.

To the clerk: I gather the General had a wee spot of bother not so long back. Two Regiment weren't best pleased when their pay didn't turn up but his nibs said it was a holy war so they should be happy to fight buckshee.

Funeral March. All look towards the rear.

The Chaplain That's the file past the body now.

Mother Courage I feel sorry for generals and emperors and the likes of them. They've their minds set on such lofty notions that folk will talk about in later days and that they'll get statues put up to themselves for. Conquerin the world, aw the rest of it, you wouldny expect these folk to think any different. These biscuits have been got at by worms... They put their whole mind into such ideas then the common folk they rely on screw everything up cause all they want is a bit of drink and a good time with their mates. No time for the bigger picture. The best laid schemes gang aft agley because of the mice that have to carry them out. Even emperors canny do it all for themselves. They have to rely on soldiers and the folk round about to get the job done, is that not correct?

The Chaplain *Laughs.* Too true Mother Courage, though I beg to differ about the the common soldier. These men do the job they're trained to do and to the best of their ability. See those squaddies standing out there in the rain drinking. I'd put my trust in them to fight for a hundred years if need be, war after war, multiple war if it came to it. And I'm no general.

Mother Courage Seventeen leather belts. You don't see any end to this war then, do you?

The Chaplain Because a general's no longer with us? Behave yourself. They're ten a penny. An endless supply of heroes.

Mother Courage I wasn't wondering just for the sake of it. It's just I'm not sure if this is the time to for me get in stock. Things are cheap at the minute, but if this war were to come to an end the bottom would fall right out the market.

The Chaplain I can see that bothers you. Well you will always get folk who say the war's got to come to an end some day. But I don't think that's the case at all. You might get what you could call a brief hiatus, a sort of breathing space till the war gathers some fresh wind; or some unexpected mishap could throw a bit of grit in its otherwise perfect functioning. We live in an imperfect world, the perfect war is nowhere to be found. It could of a sudden plunge to a juddering halt mired in all kinds of difficulties, and a good shove is needed to get it back on the road. That's where your popes and your kings and your emperors come in. They'll soon put their shoulders to the wheel. They can't do without war, and war can't do without them. It's got a long and healthy life ahead of it.

A Soldier *Sings at the counter:*

A drink quick landlord, if you please
a trooper isny long at ease
he has to fight his country's enemies.

Make that a double. I'm on holiday now.

Mother Courage If I thought you were telling me the truth…

The Chaplain Think about it. What's going to stop the war now?

The Soldier *Offstage:*

> Your tits quick lassie, if you please
> a trooper isny long at ease
> He has to ride against his enemies.

The Clerk *Suddenly:* What about peace? I'm from Bohemia. I'd like to get home every now and again.

The Chaplain Would you indeed. Ah, yes, peace perfect peace. I'm afraid you can't find the hole in a doughnut once you've scoffed it.

The Soldier *Offstage.*

> Trump cards here, comrade, if you please
> a trooper isny long at ease
> He has to end a game to fight for victory.

> Confess me, father, if you please
> a trooper isny long at ease
> He must for king and country die at peace.

The Clerk You can't get by without peace at the end of the day.

The Chaplain Well there's always a bit of peace within a war, you'll come on these little islands of peace within the conflict. War's got something for everybody, it couldn't possibly keep going without that. One performs one's basic bodily functions at stool just as much in war as in peace, between one battle and another a man can snatch a peaceable beer, even on the march one can sometimes snatch a little shuteye, chin cupped on one's elbow in a handy ditch. Of course there's no gin rummy gets played while you're assaulting the enemy, but farmers can't play gin rummy when they're ploughing their fields either can they? It's when victory comes that opportunity comes knocking on the door. True perhaps you've had a leg blown off and you may feel like causing a stink about that. But then somebody gives you a stiff brandy and you say to yourself What the heck, before you know it you're hobbling around quite the thing none the worse for war and war none the worse for you. And you know, 'Go forth and multiply' wasn't just aimed at civvy street. There's lots of multiplying gets done when your squaddie goes forth behind a barn or some other bolthole, you can't keep a good squaddie down. So the infantry breeds some infants, and on it goes. All's fair in love and war don't they say? Why on earth should all this end?

Kattrin has stopped working. She stares at the Chaplain.

Mother Courage Ok I'll take your word for it, I will stock up.

Kattrin suddenly bangs a basket of glasses down on the ground and runs out.

Mother Courage laughs. Kattrin! God struth she's her heart set on peace comin. I told her she's sure to get a man when peace comes.

She runs after her.

The Clerk *Standing up.* My game. You were too busy talking. Pay up.

Mother Courage *Returning with Kattrin.* Don't get daft ideas, the war'll last just a wee bit longer, we can raise a bit more money while it does, then peace will be all the better with more money to spend in it. Away into town, it's just ten minutes, collect the stuff from the Golden Lion. Just the dearer things we'll pick up the rest later in the wagon. It's all fixed up, the clerk here can go with you. Most of the soldiers are at the general's funeral so no harm's going to come your way. See you do this right and don't lose any of the stuff. Think of the new rigout you'll get when the time comes.

Kattrin ties a cloth round her head and exits with the clerk.

The Chaplain You're not worried about her going with the clerk?

Mother Courage With her looks she's safe enough from harm.

The Chaplain I have to hand it you Mother Courage you always stick at it and land on your feet in the end. I can see why they call you Courage.

Mother Courage It's the poor needs courage, lost souls that they are. Getting out a bed in the morning's courageous enough in their place. Or ploughin fields with a war raging round about. Even bringin a new wean into the world when mother and wean haven't a thing to look forward to. It's the poor gets asked to carry out the executions on each other, one at a time, or to shoot one another by the thousand. No wonder it can take a bit of courage for them to look one another in the face. As for their popes and emperors, it takes no small courage putting up with them when it's them that'll cost you your life in the end.

She sits, takes a small pipe form her pocket and smokes it.

Chop me a bit of wood.

The Chaplain *Reluctantly taking his coat off and preparing to chop wood.* I'm a shepherd of souls, not a hewer of wood.

Mother Courage I don't have a soul but I could do with some wood for the fire.

The Chaplain What's with the little pipe?

Mother Courage It's just a pipe.

The Chaplain I think it's a quite specific pipe.

Mother Courage Oh?

The Chaplain It belongs to cook. Two Regiment cook.

Mother Courage If you knew that in the first place what's the humming and hawing about?

The Chaplain Because I'm not sure you've *known* just whose pipe you've been smoking. Maybe you just absent- mindedly picked it up when you were rummaging through your things.

Mother Courage Maybe that's what I did.

The Chaplain I don't think so. You do know whose pipe it is.

He brings the axe down with a crash.

Mother Courage So what.

The Chaplain Allow me to perform my bounden office of advisor to you Mother Courage. That you are unlikely to see said gentleman again is no pity, but your good fortune. He did not impress me with his trustworthiness. The reverse.

Mother Courage Is that right? He struck me as a right nice fella.

The Chaplain Hmm. So he is what you call 'a right nice fellow'. I wouldn't.

The axe falls again.

Not that I would wish to demean him in any way, but 'nice' is not, definitely not, the word for him. 'Lady's man' perhaps, an underhand lady's man. Look at the pipe! It tells its own story!

Mother Courage I don't see anything special about it. Eh, *used* I suppose.

The Chaplain The stem's practically bitten right through! Such passion in a 'right nice fellow', the pipe of a man of pentup passion! Anyone with eyes in their head can see that!

He deals the block a tremendous blow.

Mother Courage You're biting right through my chopping block!

The Chaplain As aforementioned, I am no hewer of wood but a shepherd of souls. My vocation and God-given talents are here misused in physical toil, and that is a sin. You haven't heard my preaching. With one sermon I can fill a regiment with such fire its men see the enemy as nought but sheep and their own lives so disposable as outworn footwear before the prospect of final victory. God has imbued my spirit with the soul of an orator. My sermons so affect persons they know not where they are nor what time of day it is.

Mother Courage Fat lot of good that. I like to know where I am and what time of day it is.

The Chaplain It has often struck me Mother Courage that your blunt ways of speech are a mask for the softer points of your personality. You are but human. We need warmth.

Mother Courage We need warmth right enough but we'll no get it till you finish chopping that firewood.

The Chaplain That's changing the subject. Really, my dear Courage, I sometimes ponder upon what it would it be like if only you and I were to *cement* this relationship of ours that the vortex of war has so curiously placed us together in.

Mother Courage The cement seems set enough to me as it is. I cook the meals and you see to odds and ends – like chopping firewood for instance.

The Chaplain *Going over to her, gesturing with the axe.*

You know well enough what I mean by 'this relationship of ours'. Cooking and firewood and suchlike is not what I'm driving at. Make space for your feelings, woman!

Mother Courage Keep your distance from me with the axe if you please. Our relationship's too close for my liking with *that* in your hand.

The Chaplain Don't make light of this. I'm perfectly serious. I have thought this through.

Mother Courage My dear Chaplain, please get a grip of yourself. I like you well enough and wouldny want to hurt your feelins. But all I can think about the now is gettin myself and my children through the war in that wagon. The wagon isn't mine alone to worry about, I've no notion of seein about a personal life. I'm more concerned at the minute about the risk of laying out for stock when the General's dead and there's all this talk of peace in the air. Where would you go if my business went bust? Exactly. You've no idea. You just get on with that firewood and we'll manage a bit of heat the night which is enough to be grateful for times like this. What's this?

She stands up. Kattrin enters, breathless, with a wound across eye and forehead. She is dragging all sorts of articles, parcels, leather goods, a drum, etc.

What's happened, somebody attacked you? Comin back? Somebody's attacked her on the way back! I'll bet it was that manky drunk squaddie was here earlier. I should never have let you go away. Leave all that down. It's not a bad wound, only light. I'll bandage it, it'll heal within the week. Worse than animals, that's what they are.

She bandages the wound.

The Chaplain I don't just blame it all on the soldiers here. They'd never stoop to such shameful behaviour back at home. It's those who start the war are to blame, it's war brings out the lowest traits in a people.

Mother Courage Did the clerk no see you back? Suppose he thought they'd let a respectable girl like you alone. The wound isny that deep, it'll no leave a scar. There you go. That's you done. Now just hold yourself there a minute, I've something to show. A wee secret, something kept by with yourself in mind. Shut your eyes.

She digs Yvette's red boots out of a bag.

You can open them now. That's what you've aye wanted, now they're yours to keep.

She helps her to put the boots on.

Get them on you before I change my mind. That'll no show, though I'll no be sorry if it does. It's the ones they fancy the most aye comes off the worst. They haul them around with them all over the place just wearing them out. If they don't like the look a you they just let you be. I've seen a many a lovely lookin girl reduced to a sight would make the hairs on a guard dog stand on end. The girls get feart to step into the shade in the street in case something happens to them. They've an awful time of it, they really have. It's like the trees in the forest. The bonny upstanding ones are cut down for timber. The twisted ones get livin out their days in peace. This wound a yours is a stroke of luck. The boots look fine. I cleaned them up before I stored them away.

Kattrin leaves the boots and creeps into the wagon.

The Chaplain I hope she won't be left too disfigured.

Mother Courage She's goany have a scar. Peace won't improve her prospects now.

The Chaplain She never let go of any of the things she had with her.

Mother Courage Maybe I shouldn't have gone on about that so much before she went. Never know what's goin on inside that head of hers. There was the one time in years past that she stayed out all night. She never cracked a light about what happened. It used to bother me a long while thinkin about it.

She picks up the things Kattrin spilled and sorts them angrily.

War! Nice way to make your livin.

Cannon shots.

The Chaplain That's the General being lowered into his grave now. A moment in history.

Mother Courage It was a moment in history when my daughter got hit it in the face. That's her more or less on the shelf now, there's no a man'll marry her and her that's that daft about weans. It's even cause a the war she canny speak. A squaddie shoved something in her mouth when she was a wee lassie. I'll no see Swiss Cheese ever again, and God knows where Eilif is. Damn this bloody war.

Scene Seven

A road. The Chaplain, Mother Courage and Kattrin pulling the cart which is hung with new goods. Mother courage wearing a necklace of silver coins.

Mother Courage Naibdy's goany spoil my war. Wipes out your weaklings does it, well peace does that as well. Least war feeds folk.

Sings:

For all the talk of war and glory
great vict'ries won, don't kid yoursells
war's nothin but a bit of business
though no in cheese it's guns an shells.

An trying to stay in one place willny help you. They're the folk aye cop it first.

Sings:

Some folk'll look for quiet quarters
a place tae settle doon they crave
they want tae dig some hoose foundations
instead they dig an early grave.

Some rush aboot like bees oot jamjars
a peaceful spot they're searchin oot
but wance they're deid I aye jist wunnir
what aw their rush was aw aboot.

The wagon goes on its way.

Scene Eight

Camp. In front of the wagon, an old woman and her son. The son is dragging an eiderdown.

Mother Courage *From inside the wagon:* Why do you have to turn up at this hour of the morning?

Young Man We've walked all night a whole twenty miles to get here. We have to make it back home today.

Mother Courage What would I be doing with an eiderdown? Folk haveny got houses to live in!

Young Man You might at least have a look at it.

Old Woman These folk aren't interested either, come on let's go.

Young Man And end up selling the roof over our heads to pay the money we owe? Maybe she'll give us three hundred if you throw in your bracelet.

Bells start ringing.

Hear that Mum?

Voices It's peace. The king's been killed!

Mother Courage *Sticks head out the wagon. Hair still dis- shev-elled.*

What's aw the carry-on wi bells in the middle of the week?

The Chaplain *Crawling out from under the wagon.* Why the disturbance?

Mother Courage Don't tell me it's peace and I've a whole lot a new stock in!

The Chaplain *Calling:* Is it over? Has peace come?

Voices *From a distance:* The fighting stopped three weeks ago! Nobody told us!

The Chaplain Why else should they ring those bells?

Voice A whole squad of Protestants arrived with the latest news.

Young Man It's peace now Mum.

> *She collapses.*

Are you alright?

Mother Courage Holy fuck, peace! Kattrin, away get your black dress on, we'll get doon the church, Swiss Cheese is due that at least. Is this really what's happened?

Young Man The folk here are saying the same thing. It's over.

It's peace.
Are you able to stand up?

The old woman stands, dazed.

That wee saddle shop of ours will be back on its feet again as busy as ever, I'll see to that. It'll all be hunky-dory again, Dad'll get his eiderdown back. Are you able to walk now?

To the Chaplain: She took a turn there, the news was too much for her. She never thought she'd see peace again. Dad always said it would come though.

We'll away home now.

They exit.

Mother Courage *Off:* Give her a brandy.

The Chaplain They've gone already.

Mother Courage *Still off:* What's happening at the camp?

The Chaplain They all seem to be gathering. I'd better make my presence felt. Do you think it appropriate for me to re-don clerical attire?

Mother Courage Better make sure the war's really over or you might be turnin up as the anti-Christ. Peace is ok by me though even if it does clean me oot. At least two of ma children have survived, I'll get seein Eilif again.

The Chaplain And just look who we have coming from the camp now! It's cook!

The Cook *Bedraggled, carrying a bundle.* If it isn't the man of God himself! The padre!

The Chaplain Mother Courage, we have a visitor!

Mother Courage clambers out.

The Cook Well, I did say I'd come and carry on that wee blether of ours when I got the time again. And I didn't forget the brandy Mrs Fierling.

Mother Courage God almighty the Commander's cook. After all these years. Where's Eilif my oldest?

The Cook Isn't he here yet? He left in front of me, said he's on his way over here.

The Chaplain Yes, I *shall* don my clerical attire. Back in a moment. *Goes.*

Mother Courage Should be here any time now then. *Calls towards wagon.* Kattrin, Eiliff 's comin! And get a wee brandy for the cook!

Kattrin doesn't come.

Pull your hair down across your forehead and get on with it, it's no as if Mr Lamb's a stranger here.

She gets the brandy herself.

She's no comin out. Peace isny goany sort her problems, it took too long to get here. She got hit just above her eye. You'd hardly notice it but she thinks the whole world's starin at her.

The Cook Aye. War. Right enough.

He and Mother Courage sit.

Mother Courage You've come at a bad time you know. I'm done for.

The Cook How come? That's awful.

Mother Courage This peace has shafted me. I listened to the Chaplain there's advice and got in a whole new supply a stock. Now everybody's buggerin off, and I'm stuck with it.

The Cook What made you listen to *him?* If those Catholics hadn't suddenly attacked that last time we were talking, I was going to tell you to get shot of him. He's a total piss-artist. Indispensable now is he!

Mother Courage He just does the dishes and helps pull the wagon.

The Cook Pull does he! He'll have given you the benefit of of those jokes of his. His attitude to women leaves a lot to be desired. I've tried to put him right on that score but it was no use. He's got no solidity of character in him.

Mother Courage Have you got solidity of character?

The Cook I have that, if nothing else. Cheers!

Mother Courage I've only ever had the wan man had solidity
a character and he was worse than the rest a thim. I'd to
work masell to the bone for him, and he'd sell the wean's
blankets aff their beds as soon as he said it was Spring and
therefore warm enough for them. I couldny even get pla-
yin ma mooth organ, that was supposed to be 'un- Christian'. You're no makin a great case for yourself if it's solidity
a character you're blawin aboot.

The Cook Fight tooth and nail, eh. I like that in you.

Mother Courage Dream about my teeth and nails now do you.

The Cook Well it's very nice sitting here just listening to peacetime bells and you dishing out that estimable brandy of
yours.

Mother Courage I don't see what's great about peacetime bells.
I don't suppose they'll get the men their arrears of wages.
And how are they going to buy my so-called estimable
brandy without that? Has *your* regiment had all its wages
yet?

The Cook *Hesitating:* Well, not really. That's how we started
to break up. I just thought, what's the point of hanging
around here anymore, I'll go off and see an old pal or two.
So here I am.

Mother Courage To cut a long story short–you're skint!

The Cook *Annoyed by the bells:* I wish they'd stop that bloody
racket! I wouldn't mind setting up some little business for
myself, I'm pissed off being an army cook trying to knock
up meals out of tree roots and old shoe leather, getting the

scalding soup chucked back in my face. Just a dog's life that all it is. I'd quite like getting some actual fighting done, but even that's out the window now what with peace coming along.

The Chaplain turns up.

We can discuss this more later on.

The Chaplain Tolerably decent, eh? Just the occasional moth hole…

The Cook I can't see what you're getting yourself all rigged out for. You're not going to find a job with that. Who are you going to inspire now to be worthy of their hire and lay down their lives? And I've a bone to pick with you telling this woman to get all stocked up with new stuff as if the war was going to go on forever and a day.

The Chaplain *Hotly:* What conceivable business is this of yours?

The Cook It's right out of order, that's what it is! Who are you to hand out advice that's not wanted? Poking your nose in other people's business affairs!

The Chaplain And just who is 'poking their nose in' now?

To Mother Courage: I was unaware you were an intimate of this gentleman and were thus responsible to him on matters of personal import.

Mother Courage Get a grip. The cook's just chipping in his tuppence worth. You have to admit the war has proved a duff investment in the end.

The Chaplain You blaspheme the dove of peace. You would scavenge on the bodies of the brave!

Mother Courage I would *what?*

The Cook Watch your mouth my friend, or you'll get a bunch of five in it.

The Chaplain I am not parleying with you, one can see only too clearly your intentions round here.

To Mother Courage: When I see you lifting up the word 'peace' twixt finger and thumb like a used handkerchief, the humanity within me is disgusted! It lets it be seen that you want war, not peace, and this for the profit that accrues to you. Be mindful of the old saw: he who sups with the devil must use a long spoon!

Mother Courage I've nay use for war and it has little enough use for me. And if you're callin me a scavenger you can get off your mark.

The Chaplain Then why complain about peace when everyone else is relieved? Is it for the junk in your wagon?

Mother Courage They clothes and stuff kept me goin, and you too till now.

The Chaplain In war indeed! Aha!

The Cook *To the Chaplain:* Someone your age should know better than to swan around dishing out advice to other folk.

To Mother Courage: As things stand you'd be better offloading stuff right away before prices start hitting the floor. Get yourself together and wagons roll, it's not the time for hanging around.

Mother Courage Now you're talkin. Sounds sense to me.

The Chaplain Because the cook says so.

Mother Courage And how you could you no have? He's right enough, I'll get myself to the market!

She goes inside the cart.

The Cook Seems I won that one eh Chaplain? You've not got your wits about you. You should have just said, 'I wasn't offering advice, I was just discussing the political situation.' You shouldn't try taking me on. Cockfighting doesn't suit that dog's collar.

The Chaplain If you do not keep your mouth shut, I will murder you, whatever *that* suits!

The Cook *Taking his boots off:* If war hadn't turned you into such an irreligious waster you could have got yourself a manse in peacetime no bother. People don't need cooks when there's no food, but they tend to hold onto their religion whatever happens.

The Chaplain I must ask you Mr Lamb, not to elbow me out of this setup. Since I have been in poverty, I have become the better person for it. I doubt I could preach now to others.

Yvette enters all dressed up with a cane. Older, fatter, heavily powdered. Behind her a servant.

Yvette Good morning everybody! Is this Mother Courage's establishment?

The Chaplain Indeed it is. With whom have we the honour?

Yvette Madame Colonel Starhemberg, my good man. Where is Mother Courage?

The Chaplain Madame Colonel Starhemberg would like a word.

Mother Courage *Inside:* I'll be right there!

Yvette It's Yvette here!

Mother Courage *Still inside:* Ach for goodness sake, Yvette!

Yvette I've come to see you how're getting on!

> *Cook turns round in horror.*

> Peter!

The Cook Yvette!

Yvette Who would have thought it. What are you doing here?

The Cook I came on the cart.

The Chaplain Goodness me. You two are friends. *Intimate* friends?

Yvette You bet your life. *Scrutinising the cook.* You've put on the weight.

The Cook You're no celebrity model yourself.

Yvette It's good to catch up with you, swine that you are. I can tell you at last exactly what I think of you.

The Chaplain Do give him the benefit of your tongue but wait till Mother Courage is here.

Mother Courage *Comes out laden with goods.* Yvette! *They embrace.*

> What's wi aw the black?

Yvette Do you not think it's *me?* My husband the colonel passed away a few years back.

Mother Courage Thon auld buffer who near bought you the wagon?

Yvette His big brother.

Mother Courage You've done all right for yourself then. Good to see *somebody's* got a turn out the war.

Yvette Up and down, up...

Mother Courage Say what you like aboot colonels they know how to make a few bob.

The Chaplain *To the cook:* Better get your shoes on.

To Yvette: You promised to tell us what you think of this gentleman here.

The Cook Now look Yvette, just keep your hair on.

Mother Courage This bloke's a pal of mine.

Yvette That's Pete the Pipe – that's who *that* is!

The Cook Lamb's the name, cut out the nickname stuff.

Mother Courage *Laughing:* Pete the Pipe? God's gift to women? I've been holding on to his pipe for him!

The Chaplain And smoking it into the bargain.

Yvette I can put you right about that character. He's a letch. You won't find a sleazier grope on the coast of Flanders. A girl in trouble for every finger on that bastard's hands.

The Cook That's old history, it's not the way things are any more.

Yvette On your feet when you're addressing a lady! To think I used to love that man. And him all along two-timing me with a bandy little brunette. And got her up the spout needless to say.

The Cook At least it looks like I brought *you* some luck!

Yvette Shut it, creep-features! Keep your distance Mother Courage, sleazeballs like him only get worse the older they get.

Mother Courage *To Yvette:* Come with me, I'm off to get shot of this stuff before prices get any lower. Maybe with your contacts you could give us a hand with the Regiment.

Shouts into the wagon: Kattrin, forget about the church, we're away to the market! When Eilif shows up give him a drink!

Yvette Horrible to think a creep like that could have led me off the straight and narrow! Thank my lucky stars I still made something out myself eventually. I've put a stop to your game now, Mr Pete the Pipe, I'll get my reward for that in another world!

She leaves with Mother Courage.

The Chaplain This morning's text it would seem is 'The mills of God grind slowly'. And you are the one who would complain of my jokes...

The Cook I've *always* been down in my luck. Tell you the truth I was hoping for a decent hot meal here. Now she'll be sizing me up and my name will be mud. I reckon I should scarper before she comes back.

The Chaplain I think so too.

The Cook You know something Chaplain, I've had peace up to here. As far as I'm concerned we were born to put up with fire and sword, because we're born in sin. I wish I was roasting a nice fat chicken for that commander, God knows where he is. Mustard sauce, small yellow carrots...

The Chaplain Red cabbage. Red cabbage goes with chicken.

The Cook True enough. But he liked his yellow carrots.

The Chaplain He lacked comportment.

The Cook You always managed to shovel some down yourself.

The Chaplain With reluctance.

The Cook You have to admit, they were the days.

The Chaplain I would perhaps allow you that.

The Cook Since you've called her a scavenger maybe your own days are numbered round here as well. What are you staring at?

The Chaplain Eilif!

Eilif enters followed by two soldiers. His hands are fettered. He is pale.

What is going on?

Eilif Where's mum?

The Chaplain Gone into town.

Eilif They said she'd be here. I was to get a last visit.

The Cook *To the soldiers:* Where's he being taken to?

The Soldier Somewhere unpleasant.

The Chaplain What has he been doing?

The Soldier He raided a farm. The farmer's wife's a goner.

The Chaplain What brought this behaviour about?

Eilif I've done the same before.

The Cook Right, but that was *war* then.

Eilif You just shut it. Ok to sit down till she comes?

The Soldier No.

The Chaplain In war he was honoured for such behaviour, given a seat at his Commander's right hand. Bravery they called it then. Maybe I should have a word with the chief of the military police.

The Soldier You'd be wastin your time. He was stealing cattle from peasants, where's the bravery in that?

The Cook Totally stupid.

Eilif If I'd been really stupid I'd have let myself go hungry you fucking arsehole.

The Cook You were so brainy you've now to pay for it with your life.

The Chaplain We ought at least to get Kattrin out. Eilif Leave her in peace. Just give me a drop of brandy. The Soldier You've no time for that. Get moving.

The Chaplain What are we supposed to say to your mother?

Eilif Tell her there was no difference, it was just the same as the last time. Or just don't bother saying anything.

The soldiers take him away.

The Chaplain Let me be at your side on this difficult journey.

Eilif I have no need of clergy.

The Chaplain That remains to be seen.

He follows.

The Cook *Calling after him:* I'll need to tell her! She'll be wanting to see him!

The Chaplain Say nothing. At most just say he was here and he will return again, perhaps tomorrow. I will come back and report the position meantime.

He leaves quickly. The cook looks after him, shaking his head, then walks about uneasily. Approaches the wagon.

The Cook Hello in there! Do you not want to come out? I think I'm with you, you just want to hide yourself away from peace now it's here. I'm the same actually. I'm the commander's cook, remember me? Do you maybe have something in there I could eat while we're waiting on your mother? A bit of bacon or some bread even would help the time go by.

He looks in.

She's her head under a blanket.

Sound of cannon.

Mother Courage *Runs in out of breath with all her goods:* Cook, that's the peace done now, it's been war again for three days! I didny get shot a this gear after all, thank God for that! There's one of their 'firefights' goin on in the town.

We'd better clear off wi the wagon. Pack up Kattrin! What's wrang wi your face – something up?

The Cook Nope.

Mother Courage Aye there is. Can tell by the look of you.

The Cook Maybe it's with war breaking out again. Be tomorrow night I suppose before I get a decent meal now.

Mother Courage You're not being straight wi me, cook.

The Cook Eilif came. But he'd to go on right away.

Mother Courage Here was he? Ach well we'll just have to catch up with him on the march. I'll be travelling with our own side now. And how was he looking?

The Cook Same as always.

Mother Courage That yin'll never change. War'll never be able to take *him* away from me. He's got brains. Give us a hand with this packing.

She begins the packing.

And what did he have to say for himself? Still hobnob-bin wi the commander is he? Did he have any more of his heroic deeds to tell you about?

The Cook *Glumly:* I gather he's been involved in another one.

Mother Courage You can fill me in on that later, we'd better get moving.

Kattrin appears.

That's the peace over Kattrin, we're on our way again.

To the cook: What about yourself?

The Cook Think I'll join up again.

Mother Courage I suppose you could. Where's the Chaplain?

The Cook Gone into town with Eilif.

Mother Courage Why don't you just come with us, I could do with a hand.

The Cook What about the tales Yvette's been giving you?

Mother Courage No skin off ma nose. *Au contrair* dearie. Nay smoke withoot fire. You comin?

The Cook I wouldn't say no.

Mother Courage Twelve Regiment's already on its way. Take the shaft. Here's a bit of bread for you. We want to get behind the Protestant lines. With a bit of luck I'll see Eilif the night. That boy's the light of my eye. A wee blink of peace and it's back on the road.

She sings while the cook and Kattrin get themselves in harness:

From here to there, from there tae aw place
Courage's cart will aye be seen
The war needs guns tae fill its bawface
For guns an bullets always keen!
But guns an bullets willny fill it
Its regiments they still need you
so join the ranks, get to your billet
sign up yir name tae fight the noo!

Scene Nine

Two years later. Outside a halfruined parsonage. Mother Courage and the cook shabbily dressed drawing the cart.

The Cook It's all dark. Nobody up.

Mother Courage But it's a parsonage. The parson'll need to get out his feather bed to ring his bells. Then he'll be tuckin into some hot soup.

The Cook You reckon? The whole village's burnt down, seen it with our own eyes.

Mother Courage Somebody's in there, there was a dog barkin a while ago.

The Cook If the parson's got anything he'll give away bugger all.

Mother Courage Maybe we could sing for our supper...

The Cook I've had enough of this. *Suddenly:* I'd a letter from Utrecht, my mother's died of cholera. The family pub's mine now. There's the letter there if you don't believe it. You can read it all even if it is none of your business my aunt chuntering on about how I conduct my own life.

Mother Courage I'm wearied out haulin around all over the place myself. I'm like some butcher's dog draggin meat round the customers and never getting a bit itself. I've nothin worth sellin and folk havny the money to pay for it if I had. In Saxony a poor buddy in rags tried to dump all his antiquarian books on me for a couple of eggs. In Wurtemberg it's a plough yi get offered for a packet of salt. What could anybody dae wi a plough these days? There's nothin but nettles. There's one place they even say the folk in the village were for eatin the youngest weans. Even nuns are caught tryin tae loot.

The Cook It's all up with the world.

Mother Courage Sometimes I think it's like trying to cross Hell in a covered wagon selling brimstone, or goin through Heaven tryin to flog indulgences tay sinners. If only me and my children that's left could find someplace where there wisny shells an bullets flyin around, where we might get a couple of years peace and quiet.

The Cook The pair of us could open that pub. Give that some thought Anna. I've slept on it you know and decided I'm for going back even if I'm going on my own. And I mean today.

Mother Courage I'd need to speak to Kattrin. It's a bit all-of-a-sudden, and I don't like making a decision when I'm feelin the cold and there's nothing in my stomach.

Kattrin emerges from the wagon.

Kattrin, I've a thing to tell you. Cook and me fancy makin it to Utrecht, he's been left a pub there. You would have a solid base where you could get to know some folk. And any decent man would want a respectable woman like you, appearances areny everythin. I think it'd be a good idea. Cook and I rub along fine thegither, I have to say, he's got a good business head on his shoulders. We could count on our food there and that would be no bad thing, eh? You'd have your own bed to stretch yourself out in, alright? It's no bloody use this you spendin your whole life on the road. You've a heid crawlin wi lice for a start. We'd better come to a decision straight off though otherwise we're just headin north wi the Swedish troops. They'll be somewhere over there.

She points left.

I think we're at make-your-mind-up time, Kattrin.

The Cook Anna, a word. On your own.

Mother Courage Away in the wagon a minute Kattrin.

Kattrin goes back in.

The Cook I had to butt in there, you seem to be getting the wrong idea. I thought I was gettin over the picture clear enough without having to spell it out but that doesn't seem to be the case. I'll have to put my cards plain enough on the table. No way can she be coming with us. Understand?

Kattrin is listening with her head out the wagon.

Mother Courage You mean, I'd have to leave Kattrin behind?

The Cook What do you think. There isn't the room for her in the pub, it's not big enough to carry three staff. If we wire in we can make it support two of us, but never three. That's not a starter. Kattrin can keep the wagon.

Mother Courage I was hoping we would find a man for her in Utrecht.

The Cook You're joking. How's *she* going to land a husband? She's dumb with a scar into the bargain! And she's no chicken!

Mother Courage Keep your voice down.

The Cook That's the way the land lies whether my voice is down or not. It's another reason she couldn't work in the bar. Customers wouldn't fancy having somebody the likes of her in front of their eyes all day, you couldn't really blame them.

Mother Courage Just shut that mouth of yours. I told you to be quieter.

The Cook There's a light on in the parsonage. We could do our singing now.

Mother Courage Cook, how's she supposed to pull the wagon on her own? She's scared a the war. She canny stand it. The nightmares it gives her. I hear the moans of her durin the night, especially just after there's a battle. I hate to think what's she sees in they dreams. It's that hankerin to pity she's got, it gives her a hard time. Just the other day I came on a hedgehog she'd planked after we ran it over.

The Cook The pub's too small. Calls out: Gentlemen, servants, anybody inside! We're going to sing the song of Solomon, Julius Caesar and other famous folk who ended up in hard times! Understand we are just decent people who have come on hard times ourselves especially with this winter!

Sings:

You've heard of sage old Solomon
and what of him befell
that man knew all there was to know
yet he hated the day and hour of his birth
and said all things were just a show.
So great and wise was Solomon
but it's for sure as night turns day
folk could see clearly what the trouble was
twas all his wisdom had him end that way
it seems you're better off with none!

So the song demonstrates, to show you have good qualities can be dangerous in this world. Better a comfy life with a hot breakfast like a plate of soup to which I would not say no. But I'm just a soldier, what use was all that bravery fighting for my country, I've nothing to show for it but an empty stomach. Might as well just crapped it and stayed at home! What's the point?

You've heard of Julius Caesar brave
And what of him befell
they made that man into a god
but then they murdered him as well
for none this so brave man would save
him Brutus stabbed –'You too my son?'
but it's for sure as night turns day
folk could see clearly what the trouble was
twas all his bravery'd had him end that way
it seems you're better off with none!

Under his breath: They're not even looking out. *Aloud:* Gentlemen, anybody inside! Alright bravery might not put grub in a man's belly, but what about honesty then? Surely you deserve your food with that! Well, what happens?

You'll know of honest Socrates
he always spoke the truth
you'd think that he'd be thanked for that
but no, they found him evil, handed him
a glass of hemlock as his drink.
How honest was this people's son!
but it's for sure as night turns day
folk could see clearly what the trouble was
twas all his honesty'd had him end that way
it seems you're better off with none!

Share and share alike folk say, but what if you've nothing left to share? And folk that do share, if they give away all they've got they suffer as well. Charity's hard to come by, there's no profit in it!

The holy Martin was so kind
he could not need ignore
he saw a poor man in the snow
and he gave his coat to him, what's more
they simply froze to death, the two of them.
Not here on earth did he get thanks.

Well that's it. We're lawabiding citizens here, we keep to ourselves, we don't loot, murder or burn places to the ground! We're just going to sink lower and lower like the song says. No soup for us! Maybe we could fill our stomachs by robbing and looting! Crime seems to pay these days, virtue certainly doesn't! That's the way it is, but it shouldn't be!

Voice *From above:* Come on up, there's some soup here for you!

Mother Courage I couldny swallow a thing, Lamb. I wouldny say you were bein unreasonable in what you were offerin there, but is that your last word? We aye understood one another.

The Cook Last word. Think about it.

Mother Courage I've nay need to think aboot it. I'm no leavin her here.

The Cook Senseless that. But I can't alter the situation, I'm not being a monster the pub's just not big enough. We'd better get up there now or there'll be nothing to show for all this singing.

Mother Courage I'll get Kattrin.

The Cook We'd be as well taking some back for her. They'd maybe get a shock if the three of us turned up.

Both exit.

Kattrin climbs out the cart with a bundle, looks around to check the other two have gone then puts a pair of the cook's trousers and a skirt of her mother's side by side on a wheel of the cart where they will be easily seen. She finishes and is packing up her bundle to go when Mother Courage returns.

Mother Courage *With a plate of soup:* Kattrin! Hold on a minute! Where do you think you're goin with that bundle? Have you lost the place awthegither?

She looks in the bundle.

Packed aw her stuff. Are you listenin to me madam! I tellt him to get lost, he could stuff his wee pub, whut would we want wi one a them anyway? It's nay place for the likes of us. There's a lot to be earned oot this war yet.

She sees the trousers and skirt.

What an eejit. What was I supposed to do comin on this stuff and you away?

She holds Kattrin back who is trying to break away.

And don't think it's on your account I geen him his marchin orders. It's that wagon, that's aw that matters. I'm no gettin separated fray that wagon I've been used to aw these years. I've only done it for the wagon. We'll away the opposite direction, fling that cook's stuff oot here where he can pick it up himself the daft numpty.

*She climbs in and throws a few other articles in the direction
of the trousers.*

That's him got his jotters fair and square, I'll no be takin
another one on in a hurry. It's you and me now Kattrin.
This winter'll pass soon enough just like the rest a them.
Right, let's get hitched up then. Looks like snaw.

They hitch themselves to the cart and pull it away.

When the cook arrives he looks blankly at his kit.

Scene Ten

A year later. Mother Courage and Kattrin pulling the wagon. A prosperous looking farmhouse. Someone singing inside. They stop to listen.

Voice We had such roses planted
here in our garden gay
with lovely flowers blooming
which from March began to grow
and now bloom a lovely spray!
Happy those who a garden grow
With lovely flowers blooming!

When snowy blizzards swarming
go howling through the trees
we live here right contented
beneath a roof cemented
with straw and moss firm thatched.
And well that roof does keep us warm
when snowy blizzards swarm.

Mother Courage and Kattrin move on again.

Scene Eleven

A year later. The wagon much the worse for wear beside a farm-house with a huge thatched roof. It is night.

Lieutenant and three soldiers enter.

Lieutenant Totally quiet. Anybody makes a noise gets bayoneted.

First Soldier We'll need to chap them up to find out where we are.

Lieutenant That's ok, knocking on a door can sound natural, a cow bumping against a shed or something.

The soldiers knock at the farmhouse door. A peasant woman opens. A hand is clapped over her mouth. Two soldiers enter.

Man's Voice *Within:* What is it?

The soldiers bring out a peasant who is the woman's husband and their son.

Lieutenant *Points at cart where Kattrin's head has appeared.*

There's another.

A soldier drags her out.

Is this everybody that lives here?

The Peasants *Alternating:* That's our son. That's a dumb girl her mother's in town buying up stuff, the shops are closing and selling off cheap. They travel with army supplies.

Lieutenant Keep it down. I'm telling you, one sound and your heads are split open with this weapon. Somebody needs to show the way to the town. *Points to the young peasant:* Right, here you!

Young Peasant I don't know the way.

Second Soldier Grinning: He doesn't know the way!

Young Peasant I'm not into helping Catholics.

Lieutenant *To the Second Soldier:* Give him your bayonet in him.

Young Peasant *Forced to his knees, the bayonet at his throat.* I'll die before I tell you!

Second Soldier *Again mimicking:* He'll die before he tells us!

First Soldier I think I know what might change his mind.

Walks over to the cowshed.

Two cows and an ox. OK, if you can't be reasonable, these animals are for my bayonet.

Young Peasant Aw, not our livestock.

Peasant's Wife *Weeping:* You kill them we'll starve!

Lieutenant That's what he gets for being so obstinate.

First Soldier I suppose I could start with the ox.

Young Peasant *To his father:* Should I?

His mother nods.

Ok I'll show you.

Peasant Wife Oh thanks very much captain for letting us live, we'll be eternally grateful to you. Thank you. Thank you.

The peasant stops his wife from going on thanking him.

First Soldier I was right the ox'd be the one to get them!

Lieutenant and two soldiers exit led by the young peasant.

Peasant Like to know what they're planning. It'll be nothing good.

Peasant Wife Maybe they're just sussing out what's ahead. What are you up to?

Peasant *Setting a ladder against the roof, climbing up.*

I'm just going to see if they're on their own.

From the top of the ladder: There's movement over at the woods. I can see as far as the quarry. There's soldiers out in the open, they've a gun. There must be at least a whole regiment. God help that town and everybody in there.

Peasant Wife Are there any lights on in the town?

Peasant Nup. They must all be asleep. *He climbs down.* When that town gets invaded its folk'll be cut to bits.

Peasant Wife The lookout'll spot the soldiers in time.

Peasant They must have killed the watchman already up in his tower. He'd have sounded the alarm by now.

Peasant Wife If only there was more of us.

Peasant We're just stuck here with that bloody dumb one.

Peasant Wife We can't do a thing, can we?

Peasant Nothing.

Peasant Wife There's no way of getting down there in the dark.

Peasant The whole hill's crawling with army. We couldn't even try to send a signal.

Peasant Wife That would bring our own deaths on us.

Peasant Yep, there's damn all we can do.

Peasant Wife *To Kattrin:* Pray, poor thing that you are, pray! We've no way of stopping all this bloodshed, if you can't speak least you can pray. He hears on high if nobody else does. I'll lead.

All kneel, Kattrin behind the two peasants.

Our Father who art in heaven, hear our prayer that the town be spared and everybody in it lying asleep just now not knowing the danger they are in. Let them waken, get up and go to the town walls where they will see the enemy with bayonets and guns approaching this night across the fields under the hill.

Turning to Kattrin: Guard over our mother, let the town lookout not sleep but waken up or it will be too late. Help thou our son-in-law with his four children, dear God let them not be killed, they are just innocent ones.

To Kattrin, who groans: The youngest isn't even two, the oldest is seven.

Kattrin rises, troubled.

Dear father above, hear our prayer, help us or we will die. We are powerless without bayonets or anything like that, and have no one to put our trust in but you, we are in thy hands here with our farm and livestock. In thy hands too is the town before whose walls the enemy are gathering with all their might.

Unobserved Kattrin has gone to the cart and taken something out of it which she hides under her apron. She climbs the ladder onto the roof.

Please remember the children who are now at peril, even the littlest, and those elderly too frail to move, and all your creatures below.

Peasant And forgive us our trespasses as we forgive those who trespass against us. Amen.

Sitting on the roof Kattrin takes a drum from under her apron and begins drumming.

Peasant Wife Jesus, what's she up to?

Peasant She's off her head.

Peasant Wife Get her down from there quick.

The Peasant runs for the ladder but Kattrin pulls it up onto the roof.

She'll be the death of the lot of us.

Peasant Stop it, dumb idiot! Stop that drumming now!

Peasant Wife The army'll be here on top of us.

Peasant *Looking for stones:* I'll knock you off of there.

Peasant Wife Have you no pity in you? Have you no heart? We're lost if the army comes here, they'll bayonet us!

Kattrin stares into the distance towards the town. She goes on drumming.

Peasant *To her husband:* I told you we should never have let that lot into the farm. What would it matter to them even if our last beast got killed?

Lieutenant *Running back with soldiers and the young peasant.*

I'm going to have you crowd for mincemeat!

Peasant Wife We're innocent officer we couldn't stop her she sneaked up there herself. She's nobody of ours!

Lieutenant Where's the ladder?

Peasant Up there with her.

Lieutenant I command you to throw that drum down!

Kattrin continues drumming.

You're all party to this. Your number's up.

Peasant They've been felling trees in the wood there. We could get a trunk to try and dislodge her...

First Soldier *To the lieutenant:* If you'll allow me Sir I think I've an idea might do the trick.

He whispers to the Lieutenant, who nods.

Listen to me you! I've an offer for your own good! Come down out of there and take us into town! Point out your mother there and we'll spare her life!

Kattrin goes on drumming.

Lieutenant She doesn't trust you, hardly surprising with a face like yours.

Calls up to Kattrin: Will you take my word for it? I am an officer and I give you my word of honour!

Kattrin drums harder.

She holds nothing sacred.

Young Peasant Captain, this isn't just about her mother!

First Soldier It better not go on like this. The town's sure to hear her.

Lieutenant We need to drown out the drumming with something louder. What with?

First Soldier I thought the idea was to have no noise at all!

Lieutenant I mean an innocuous noise, you fool. Not a military one!

Peasant I could make a noise chopping wood with my axe.

Lieutenant Yes, get chopping!

Peasant gets an axe and begins chopping.

Harder! Chop harder! Chop as if your life depends on it!

Kattrin has been listening, and beating the drum with less force. She looks distractedly around her but continues drumming.

The sound's too weak. *To the first soldier:* You get chopping too!

Peasant There's only one axe.

He stops chopping.

Lieutenant We'd better set the house on fire. That'll smoke her out.

Peasant That'd be no use. When they saw the fire the town'd know everything.

During the drumming Kattrin has been listening. Now she laughs.

Lieutenant Thinks she can laugh at us now does she. I'm putting a stop to this. I'm going to have her shot down and that's the end of the matter. Get me a gun!

The two soldiers run off. Kattrin goes on drumming.

Peasant Wife I know what. That's their wagon there. We start smashing that up she'll soon stop. That's all they have.

Lieutenant *To the young peasant:* Start smashing it!

Calling: Stop the drumming or we wreck your wagon!

The young peasant strikes the cart a few feeble blows with a plank.

Peasant Wife *To Kattrin:* Stop that you brute!

Kattrin looks towards the cart emitting pitiful sounds. But she continues drumming.

Lieutenant What's keeping those bastards?

First Soldier The town's heard nothing or it would be sounding off its cannon.

Lieutenant *Shouting up:* They cannot hear you, and you are going to be shot now. For the last time. Throw down that drum!

Young Peasant *Drops the board, screams to Kattrin:* Keep drumming! If you don't everybody's finished! Keep drumming, keep drumming...

The soldier knocks him down and starts beating him. Kattrin starts to cry but keeps on drumming.

Peasant Wife Lay off the boy's back for God's sake you'll kill him!

The soldier rush in with the gun.

Second Soldier The colonel's livid Captain. We're going to be courtmartialled.

Lieutenant Get it ready! Set it up!

He calls while the weapon is trained on the roof.

For the last time! Stop that drumming!

In tears, Kattrin drums as loud as she is able.

Fire!

The soldiers fire the gun. Kattrin is hit. She gives some last beats on the drum then subsides slowly to a crumpled heap.

That's the end of that noise then!

But the final beats of the drum trigger the sound of cannon from the town in the distance. A rising swell of cannon and tocsin alarms.

First Soldier She's done it.

Scene Twelve

Night becoming morning. Military march music recedes. Before the cart Mother Courage with the body of her daughter. The peasants stand nearby.

Peasant *With hostility:* You'd better get on your way Missus. There's just one regiment bringing up the rear. You can't go on your own.

Mother Courage Maybe she's jist sleepin.

> *hushaby ma dearie*
> *nestlin' in the hay*
> *neighbours' weans are girnin*
> *oors jist run an play*
> *neighbours weans are clatty*
> *oors are clean an neat*
> *lookin like an angel*
> *sae sweet.*

> *neighbours weans go starvin*
> *oors have cake aw day*
> *an if their cake's too crumbly*
> *aw they need is say*
> *hushaby ma dearie*
> *nestlin in the hay*
> *I've wan lay doon in Poland*
> *the other's faur away.*

You shouldny have told her about they weans of your brother-in-law.

Peasant If you hadn't gone off bargainhunting in the town this mightn't have happened.

Mother Courage She's asleep.

Peasant Wife She's not asleep, you have to face up to it, she's gone.

Peasant And it's time you were gone yourself. There's wolves round here and bandits worse than that.

Mother Courage Aye.

She goes and gets a cloth from the wagon to cover the body.

Peasant Wife Have you nobody else? Somebody you can go to? Mother Courage Aye, still the one. My Eilif.

Peasant *As Mother Courage covers the dead girl:* You're as well go and find him then. Leave her to us, we'll see she gets a decent burial. Don't worry about that.

Mother Courage There's some money for the expenses.

She hands some money to the Peasant. He and his son shake her hand then carry Kattrin away.

Peasant Wife *Likewise grasps her hand with a farewell bow, leaves saying:*

I need to go myself, I need to go!

Mother Courage *Harnessing herself to the wagon:* I just hope I can pull this thing on my own. Aye, no bother, there's no much in it just now. I'll need to try and get this business on its feet again.

Another regiment is heard passing with marching music. Mother Courage tugs the cart.

Hoy! Take me way ye!

As she leaves, is heard the singing

Wi aw its dangers an stray bullets
this war drags on from day to day
the war could last a hundred years yet
yer common sojer willny win.
pure crap his food, his gear his rucksack
the regiment docks hauf his pay
an though it might strike you a wonder
this war will never go away!

It's springtime noo! move on your way
the snaw's aw gone. the deid lie deid
but you that huvny died as yet
the powers that be, they still do need.

www.ingramcontent.com/pod-product-compliance
Lightning Source LLC
Chambersburg PA
CBHW051436140726
47987CB00006B/2401